Workbook 1 • Lessons 1-15
basicesl.com/workbook-1

For beginner English language learners

SESMA

Basic ESL® Workbook 1
3rd Edition

Publisher:

Bilingual Dictionaries, Inc.
P.O. Box 1154
Murrieta, CA 92564
Website: www.bilingualdictionaries.com
Email: support@bilingualdictionaries.com

Original Content by C. Sesma, M.A.
English and Spanish Teacher

Revised, Designed and Edited by Bilingual Dictionaries, Inc.
Alex Sesma • Editor, Content, Design
Kevin Cole • Content, ESL Teacher
Jose Quezada • Design, Illustrations

Copyright © 2021 by Bilingual Dictionaries, Inc.
All rights reserved. No part of this book may be reproduced or transmitted in any form or by any means.

ISBN13: 978-1-946986-99-3
ISBN10: 1-946986-99-2

For **information, downloads** and **videos** please visit the Basic ESL® website:
Website: www.basicesl.com
Email: support@basicesl.com

Printed in the USA
v221003

Basic ESL Workbook

Basic ESL introduces grammar and writing to beginner English language learners. Students improve their English skills through simple examples and exercises. Each lesson includes a topic for vocabulary and introduces a basic grammar concept. The workbook exercises are built around each lesson's vocabulary and grammar examples. This provides students an opportunity to practice sentence structure and vocabulary together in a meaningful way. The workbooks are an excellent resource for students to practice writing skills and improve their English.

The 45 lessons are designed to give beginner students a lesson-by-lesson path for improving their English. Each lesson builds on the previous lesson's vocabulary and grammar. After completing all 3 workbooks, students will have covered multiple parts of speech, different tenses, modals and much more.

3 Workbooks • 45 lessons

There are three workbooks with 15 lessons each. The complete workbook series includes 45 lessons.

- Workbook 1: Lessons 1-15
- Workbook 2: Lessons 16-30
- Workbook 3: Lessons 31-45

Instructions

We encourage students to complete the lessons in order and with the help of a teacher, tutor or friend.

1. Review lesson vocabulary and grammar
2. Watch the lesson videos
3. Complete the exercises in the workbook
4. Download extra exercises

Videos and Downloads | basicesl.com | YouTube

Each workbook lesson features English pronunciation videos to practice the lesson vocabulary and grammar. The vocabulary and grammar examples in the videos are identical to the workbooks. The examples are presented in order, through an easy-to-understand listen-and-repeat format. The videos are an excellent resource for students to practice listening, reading, and speaking skills.

Extra downloads including extra exercise worksheets and lesson quizzes are also available. Visit our website to find all the extra resources that go along with each lesson. Become a basicesl.com member to download worksheets and get discount pricing on workbooks and bilingual dictionaries.

- Vocabulary Videos
- Grammar Videos
- Exercise Videos

- Vocabulary Exercises
- Grammar Exercises
- Lesson Quizzes

- Workbooks
- Dictionaries

Contact Us

Please contact us with any questions, comments or suggestions. Call or email us:

(951)-296-2445 • support@basicesl.com
Monday - Friday • 7 a.m. to 3 p.m.

Dear Teachers & Students

We thank you for your continued support. You are appreciated. Please send us any feedback or suggestions. We are listening.

We wish you the best, and a bright future!

Table of Contents

Workbook 1	**Vocabulary** • Grammar	**Page**
	Dear teachers and students	3
	List of irregular verbs	6
	basicesl.com	8

Family

Lesson 1 — **Family Members** 9
- Singular and plural nouns
- Statements with the verb *to be*
- Asking for names

Lesson 2 — **Describing People** 17
- Statements with the verb *to be* and adjectives
- Negative statements with the verb *to be*
- Asking for description

Lesson 3 — **Age** 25
- Possessive adjectives
- Contractions with the verb *to be*
- Asking for age

School

Lesson 4 — **School** 33
- Simple present statements
- Asking for location

Lesson 5 — **Classroom** 41
- Simple present negative statements
- Math statements

Lesson 6 — **School Supplies** 49
- Simple present statements with *to be*, *to have*, *to go* and *to do*
- Using the helping verb *to do* for emphasis

Table of Contents

| Workbook 1 | Vocabulary • Grammar | Page |

Home

Lesson 7 — **House** 57
    Questions with the verb *to be*
    Using question words with the verb *to be*

Lesson 8 — **Kitchen** 65
    Simple present questions
    Using question words with simple present questions

Lesson 9 — **Bedroom & Bathroom** 73
    Plural noun spelling rules
    Possessive form of nouns

Clothes

Lesson 10 — **Clothes** 81
    Using *this*, *that*, *these* and *those*
    Questions about possession with *whose*

Lesson 11 — **Style** 89
    Word substitution with *one* and *ones*
    Questions about choice with *which*
    Ordinal numbers

Lesson 12 — **Shopping** 97
    Prepositions of time and place
    Prepositions and prepositional phrases

City

Lesson 13 — **City** 105
    Present continuous statements
    Present participle spelling rules (*-ing* verb form)

Lesson 14 — **Traveling** 113
    Present continuous negative statements
    Present continuous questions

Lesson 15 — **Directions** 121
    Imperative statements
    Asking for direction

Workbook 1 — **Answer Key** 129

Irregular Verbs

Base Form	Simple Past	Past Participle
arise	arose	arisen
awake	awoke	awoken
be	was / were	been
bear	bore	born(e)
beat	beat	beaten
become	became	become
begin	began	begun
bend	bent	bent
bet	bet	bet
bind	bound	bound
bite	bit	bitten
bleed	bled	bled
blow	blew	blown
break	broke	broken
breed	bred	bred
bring	brought	brought
broadcast	broadcast	broadcast
build	built	built
burn	burnt *burned*	burnt *burned*
burst	burst	burst
buy	bought	bought
catch	caught	caught
choose	chose	chosen
cling	clung	clung
come	came	come
cost	cost	cost
creep	crept	crept
cut	cut	cut
deal	dealt	dealt
dig	dug	dug
do	did	done
draw	drew	drawn
dream	dreamt *dreamed*	dreamt *dreamed*
drink	drank	drunk
drive	drove	driven
eat	ate	eaten
fall	fell	fallen
feed	fed	fed
feel	felt	felt
fight	fought	fought
find	found	found
fit	fit	fit
fly	flew	flown
forbid	forbade	forbidden
forget	forgot	forgotten
forgive	forgave	forgiven
freeze	froze	frozen
get	got	got
give	gave	given
go	went	gone
grind	ground	ground
grow	grew	grown
hang	hung	hung
have	had	had
hear	heard	heard
hide	hid	hidden
hit	hit	hit
hold	held	held
hurt	hurt	hurt
keep	kept	kept
kneel	knelt	knelt
know	knew	known
lay	laid	laid
lead	led	led
lean	leant *leaned*	leant *leaned*
learn	learnt *learned*	learnt *learned*
leave	left	left
lent	lent	lent
lie (in bed)	lay	lain
light	lit *learned*	lit *learned*

Irregular Verbs

Base Form	Simple Past	Past Participle
lose	lost	lost
make	made	made
mean	meant	meant
meet	met	met
mow	mowed	mown *mowed*
overtake	overtook	overtaken
pay	paid	paid
put	put	put
read	read	read
ride	rode	ridden
ring	rang	rung
rise	rose	risen
run	ran	run
saw	sawed	sawn *sawed*
say	said	said
see	saw	seen
sell	sold	sold
send	sent	sent
set	set	set
sew	sewed	sewn *sewed*
shake	shook	shaken
shall	should	…
shed	shed	shed
shine	shone	shone
shoot	shot	shot
show	showed	shown
shrink	shrank	shrunk
shut	shut	shut
sing	sang	sung
sink	sank	sunk
sit	sat	sat
sleep	slept	slept
slide	slid	slid
smell	smelt	smelt
sow	sowed	sown *sowed*

Base Form	Simple Past	Past Participle
speak	spoke	spoken
spell	spelt *spelled*	spelt *spelled*
spend	spent	spent
spill	spilt *spilled*	spilt *spilled*
spit	spat	spat
spread	spread	spread
stand	stood	stood
steal	stole	stolen
stick	stuck	stuck
sting	stung	stung
stink	stank	stunk
strike	struck	struck
swear	swore	sworn
sweep	swept	swept
swell	swelled	swollen *swelled*
swim	swam	swum
swing	swung	swung
take	took	taken
teach	taught	taught
tear	tore	torn
tell	told	told
think	thought	thought
throw	threw	thrown
understand	understood	understood
wake	woke	woken
wear	wore	worn
weep	wept	wept
win	won	won
wind	wound	wound
write	wrote	written
can	could	…
may	might	…
will	would	…

Workbook 1 • Lessons 1-15

basicesl.com

Lessons = Workbooks + Videos

We provide English pronunciation videos for all of our vocabulary and grammar examples. Our videos give students a chance to listen and repeat the sentence structures found in each lesson.

Videos found on **basicesl.com** are student friendly, with no ads or commercials.

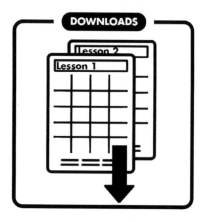

Members = Downloads + Discounts

Extra downloads are available online. Join **basicesl.com** to download additional exercises.

- Vocabulary worksheets
- Grammar worksheets
- Quiz worksheets

Member 1 = Downloads

Member 2 = Downloads + Workbooks

Member 3 = Downloads + Workbooks + Discount

Workbooks and Dictionaries

Find our workbooks and bilingual dictionaries at **basicesl.com.** Discount members receive an online shopping discount. Bilingual dictionaries are a great tool for English language learners.

Basic ESL Workbooks along with bilingual dictionaries are great tools for teachers that have ESL students with different native languages.

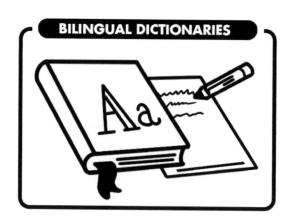

basicesl.com/workbook-1

Lesson 1

Family Members

Singular and plural nouns
Statements with subject pronouns and the verb *to be*
Indefinite and definite articles
Asking for names

 basicesl.com/workbook-1/lesson-01

☐	Watch vocabulary video. Listen and repeat.
☐	Complete vocabulary exercises. (**Download**)
☐	Watch grammar video. Listen and repeat.
☐	Complete grammar exercises. (**Workbook**)
☐	Complete extra grammar exercises. (**Download**)
☐	Take a quiz. (**Download**)

Vocabulary

1. family
2. grandmother
3. grandfather
4. grandparents
5. mother
6. father
7. parents
8. children
9. son
10. daughter
11. grandson
12. granddaughter
13. aunt
14. uncle
15. niece
16. nephew
17. brother
18. sister
19. husband
20. wife

21. cousin (*noun*)
22. in-law (*noun*)
23. friend (*noun*)
24. name (*noun*)
25. your (*adj*)
26. my (*adj*)
27. what (*adv*)
28. from (*prep*)
29. of (*prep*)

Grammar

Singular and plural nouns

son → sons	daughter → daughters
brother → brothers	sister → sisters
father → fathers	mother → mothers
nephew → nephews	niece → nieces
grandfather → grandfathers	grandmother → grandmothers
grandson → grandsons	granddaughter → granddaughters

Nouns are words used to name people, places, or things. Most plural nouns are formed by adding –s to the singular noun.

Singular means one. Plural means more than one.

Statements with subject pronouns and the verb *to be*

A subject noun is the subject of a sentence. In statements with the verb *to be*, the subject noun comes before the verb. Subject pronouns replace subject nouns.

Subject noun	Subject pronoun
Tony **is** a father.	*I* **am** a father.
Mary **is** a mother.	*You* **are** a mother.
John **is** an uncle.	*He* **is** an uncle.
Jane **is** an aunt.	*She* **is** an aunt.
Kevin **is** my name.	*It* **is** my name.
Carlos and I **are** cousins.	*We* **are** cousins.
You and Leah **are** sisters.	*You* **are** sisters.
Mark and Sarah **are** friends.	*They* **are** friends.

There are singular and plural subject pronouns.

Singular	Plural
I	we
you	you
he, she, it	they

The verb *to be* has different forms for different subjects.

I **am**	We **are**
You **are**	You **are**
He **is**	They **are**
She **is**	
It **is**	

Indefinite and definite articles

Indefinite		Definite
a sister-in-law	**an** uncle	**the** wife of Joe
a brother	**an** aunt	**the** son of Mary

Indefinite	Definite
I *am* **an** uncle.	I *am* **the** uncle of James.
You *are* **an** aunt.	You *are* **the** aunt of James.
Tom *is* **a** friend.	He *is* **the** friend of James.
Sarah *is* **a** wife.	She *is* **the** wife of James.
James *is* **a** name.	It *is* **the** name of my nephew.
Billy and I *are* **brothers**.	We *are* **the** brothers of Jane.
You and Joe *are* **grandparents**.	You *are* **the** grandparents of Jane.
Amy and Anna *are* **cousins**.	They *are* **the** cousins of Jane.

Articles are used to introduce nouns. The indefinite articles *a* and *an* are used for nouns that are not specific.

The indefinite article *an* is only used with nouns that begin with a vowel (*a, e, i, o, u*) or silent *h*.

The definite article *the* is used for specific nouns.

Asking for names

Question	Answer
What *is* your name?	My name *is* **Jim**.
What *is* your last name?	My last name *is* **Smith**.
What *is* your full name?	My full name *is* **Jim Smith**.

The question word *what* is used to ask for information. The word *what* and the verb *to be* are used to ask for names.

Workbook 1 • Lesson 1: Family Members

Exercises

A: Write the **plural** form of the **noun**.

1. sister _sisters_
2. aunt _____
3. husband _____
4. nephew _____
5. friend _____
6. niece _____
7. brother _____
8. name _____
9. mother _____
10. cousin _____
11. father _____
12. daughter _____

B: Choose the article **a** or **an**.

1. _a_ sister
2. _____ aunt
3. _____ husband
4. _____ nephew
5. _____ friend
6. _____ niece
7. _____ brother
8. _____ name
9. _____ mother
10. _____ cousin
11. _____ uncle
12. _____ daughter

C: Write the subject pronoun for the given subject.

1. sister _she_
2. sisters _____
3. Greg and I _____
4. Albert _____
5. The nieces of Tim _____
6. You and Alex _____
7. China _____
8. You and I _____

D: Write the **correct** form of **to be**.

1. he _is_
2. you _____
3. it _____
4. they _____
5. we _____
6. I _____
7. she _____
8. you and I _____

basicesl.com/workbook-1/lesson-01

Exercises

E: Fill in the blanks using names and family member vocabulary.

1. The _wife_ of _Henry_ is Sarah.

2. The sister of _____ is Amy.

3. The _____ of Henry and _____ are Ray and Lily.

4. The _____ of Sarah and _____ are _____ and Carmen.

5. The _____ of Lily is Ray.

6. The _____ of Lily are _____ and Anthony.

7. The _____ of Amy are _____ and _____.

8. The _____ of Lily and _____ is Jose.

Exercises

F: Use the clues to write three sentences. Follow the example.

1. Katie / Betty

*My name is **Katie**.*

*I am a **sister**.*

*I am the **sister** of **Betty**.*

2. Diana / Eric

My name...

I am...

I am the...

3. Walter / William

4. Paula / Bob

5. Julian / Taylor

basicesl.com/workbook-1/lesson-01

Exercises

G: Complete the sentence with the present tense form of the verb *to be:* **am**, **is**, or **are**.

1. Mary __is__ my sister.
2. You _____ my brother.
3. She _____ a mother.
4. I _____ an uncle.
5. He _____ a father.
6. They _____ friends.
7. My name _____ Henry.
8. I _____ Henry.
9. She _____ my daughter.
10. My son _____ from Mexico.
11. I _____ from India.
12. My last name _____ Smith.
13. I _____ Susan.
14. The cousins _____ from China.
15. You _____ from China.
16. We _____ a family.
17. Sue and Liz _____ sisters.
18. You _____ an uncle.
19. We _____ brothers.
20. The name of my mother _____ Liz.
21. Mary and Susan _____ friends.
22. They _____ from China.

H: Fill in the blanks using articles, subject pronouns, the verb *to be*, or family member vocabulary.

1. The sisters __are__ (am, is, are) from Mexico. Jane is _____ (a, an) friend of my brother. Jenny is _____ (a, an) aunt. She _____ (am, is, are) the aunt of my cousin.

2. My name _____ (am, is, are) Ben. I _____ (am, is, are) a grandson. My father is the _____ (family) of my grandfather. My sister is the _____ (family) of my father. My mother is _____ (a, an, the) wife of my father. _____ (I, you, he) am the son of my mother.

3. _____ (I, we, she) are cousins. The name of our grandmother _____ (am, is, are) Cecilia Gomez. We _____ (am, is, are) from the United States. My last name _____ (am, is, are) Jennings. _____ (a, an, the) last name of my cousins _____ (am, is, are) Campos.

Workbook 1 • Lesson 1: Family Members

Exercises

I: Listen to the story and choose the correct answer.
Visit **basicesl.com/workbook-1/lesson-01** to listen to the story.

1. The family of Tim is from ___Mexico___ .

   a. Mexico   **b.** China   **c.** here

2. Tony is the _____ of Tim.

   a. uncle   **b.** brother   **c.** friend

3. Steve is the _____ of Tim .

   a. father   **b.** uncle   **c.** brother

4. Mary is the _____ of Tim.

   a. aunt   **b.** sister   **c.** mother

5. Jane and Julia are _____ .

   a. cousins   **b.** sisters   **c.** brothers

6. Jane and Julia are the _____ of Tim.

   a. sisters   **b.** friends   **c.** cousins

basicesl.com/workbook-1/lesson-01

Lesson 2

Describing People

Statements with the verb *to be* and adjectives
Negative statements with the verb *to be*
Asking for description

 basicesl.com/workbook-1/lesson-02

- ☐ Watch vocabulary video. Listen and repeat.
- ☐ Complete vocabulary exercises. (**Download**)
- ☐ Watch grammar video. Listen and repeat.
- ☐ Complete grammar exercises. (**Workbook**)
- ☐ Complete extra grammar exercises. (**Download**)
- ☐ Take a quiz. (**Download**)

Vocabulary

1. tall (*adj*)	**2.** short (*adj*)	**3.** fat (*adj*)	**4.** skinny (*adj*)
5. ugly (*adj*)	**6.** beautiful (*adj*)	**7.** handsome (*adj*)	**8.** pretty (*adj*)
9. happy (*adj*)	**10.** sad (*adj*)	**11.** young (*adj*)	**12.** old (*adj*)
13. married (*adj*)	**14.** single (*adj*)	**15.** nice (*adj*)	**16.** mean (*adj*)
17. funny (*adj*)	**18.** serious (*adj*)	**19.** confident (*adj*)	**20.** shy (*adj*)

21. good (*adj*)   **22.** bad (*adj*)   **23.** smart (*adj*)

24. polite (*adj*)   **25.** rude (*adj*)   **26.** weird (*adj*)

27. honest (*adj*)   **28.** and (*conj*)   **29.** like (*prep*)

basicesl.com/workbook-1/lesson-02

Grammar

Statements with the verb *to be* and adjectives

I *am* **tall**.	You *are* **short**.
The daughters *are* **happy**.	The sons *are* **sad**.
The grandfather *is* **confident**.	The grandmother *is* **shy**.
The sister *is* **nice**.	The brother *is* **mean**.
The nieces *are* **young**.	The nephews *are* **old**.
The uncles *are* **funny**.	The aunts *are* **serious**.

Subject noun	**Subject pronoun**
John *is* smart.	**He** *is* smart.
The grandmother *is* happy.	**She** *is* happy.
China *is* nice.	**It** *is* nice.
The cousin of John *is* fat.	**He** *is* fat.
Jim and I *are* handsome.	**We** *are* handsome.
You and Mary *are* pretty.	**You** *are* pretty.
John and Sarah *are* married.	**They** *are* married.
The friends *are* smart.	**They** *are* smart.

Adjectives are words used to describe nouns. Adjectives can be placed after the verb *to be* to describe the subject.

Subject + *to be* + **adjective**.

Some adjectives have opposite meanings.

tall → short   nice → mean
young → old   good → bad

Negative statements with the verb *to be*

Statement	**Negative statement**
I *am* skinny.	I *am* **not** skinny.
You *are* pretty.	You *are* **not** pretty.
He *is* tall.	He *is* **not** tall.
They *are* good.	They *are* **not** good.

Tom *is* rude.	He *is* **not** polite.
Mary and Tom *are* married.	They *are* **not** single.
You and I *are* nice.	We *are* **not** mean.
Our last name *is* Smith.	It *is* **not** Jones.

Negative statements with the verb *to be* are formed with the word *not* after the verb *to be*.

Subject + *to be* (**not**) + adjective.

Asking for description

Question	**Answer**
What *am* I **like**?	You *are* **tall**.
What *are* you **like**?	I *am* **short**.
What *is* Sarah **like**?	She *is* **pretty**.
What *are* Tom and Tim **like**?	They *are* **handsome**.
What *is* Mexico **like**?	It *is* **beautiful**.
What *are* you and Mary **like**?	We *are* **smart**.

Use the question word *what* and the word *like* to ask for the description of a noun (person, place or thing).

What + *to be* + subject + **like**?

Workbook 1 • Lesson 2: Describing People

Exercises

A: Write the **opposite** adjective.

1. nice __mean__
2. tall _____
3. handsome _____
4. shy _____
5. married _____
6. pretty _____
7. beautiful _____
8. short _____
9. rude _____

10. skinny _____
11. funny _____
12. old _____
13. mean _____
14. happy _____
15. good _____
16. ugly _____
17. fat _____
18. bad _____

B: Write the **male** relationship. (Review)

1. wife __husband__
2. aunt _____
3. niece _____
4. mother _____
5. sister _____

6. grandmother _____
7. daughter _____
8. sister-in-law _____
9. granddaughter _____

C: Use a definite (**D**) article (*the*) or an indefinite (**I**) article (*a, an*) for each noun. (Review)

1. (D) __the__ niece
2. (I) __a__ niece
3. (D) _____ nieces
4. (D) _____ father
5. (D) _____ brothers
6. (I) _____ brother

7. (I) _____ pretty wife
8. (I) _____ honest husband
9. (I) _____ husband
10. (D) _____ happy grandmothers
11. (I) _____ ugly son
12. (I) _____ handsome uncle

basicesl.com/workbook-1/lesson-02

Exercises

D: Replace the underlined **subject** with the correct subject pronoun: *I, You, He, She, It, We, They*.

1. The **brothers** are short.   *They* are short.
2. **Mary** is not ugly.   *She* is not ugly.
3. **China** is beautiful.   _____
4. **John** is confident.   _____
5. The **uncle** is single.   _____
6. The **brothers** are handsome.   _____
7. The **niece** is shy.   _____
8. The **grandfather** is old.   _____
9. **Sara** is skinny.   _____
10. **Sara** and **Ann** are polite.   _____
11. **Tom** and **I** are smart.   _____
12. My **wife** and **I** are not happy.   _____
13. **You** and **Mike** are sad.   _____
14. The old **grandfather** is honest.   _____
15. **Pat** and **Susan** are sad.   _____
16. The **cousin** is not married.   _____
17. The confident **son** is married.   _____
18. The **grandmother** is funny.   _____
19. My **brother-in-law** is short.   _____
20. **Lee** and **Henry** are from China.   _____
21. **Henry** and **I** are brothers.   _____
22. **You** and **Mary** are married.   _____

Workbook 1 • Lesson 2: Describing People

Exercises

E: Form a **negative** statement. Use an opposite adjective.

1. She is nice.   _She is **not** mean._
2. You are tall. _____
3. She is pretty. _____
4. I am single.   _____
5. He is happy.   _____
6. They are skinny. _____
7. We are pretty. _____

F: Use the given words to from a sentence.

1. tall Pat are Steven and.   _Pat and Steven are tall._
2. nephew is The shy.   _____
3. rude not are You.   _____
4. Mary like is What?   _____
5. handsome I and tall am.   _____
6. brother is The happy not. _____
7. He not is brother my.   _____

G: Complete the sentence with to be: **am, is, are**. Make the sentence affirmative **(A)** or negative **(N)**.

1. **(A)** The cousin _is_ happy.
2. **(N)** He _is not_ sad.
3. **(A)** Sara _____ young.
4. **(N)** She _____ old.
5. **(A)** The brothers _____ nice.
6. **(N)** They _____ mean.
7. **(A)** You and I _____ short.
8. **(N)** We _____ tall.
9. **(A)** Mexico _____ beautiful.
10. **(N)** It _____ ugly.
11. **(A)** The sons _____ confident.
12. **(N)** They _____ shy.

basicesl.com/workbook-1/lesson-02

Exercises

H: Form one question and two statements. Use opposite <u>adjectives</u>. Follow the example.

1. Tom

*What is **Tom** like?*
*He is **skinny**.*
*He is **not fat**.*

2. Aunt Mary

3. Jim and Carol

4. You

5. The sisters

6. I

Workbook 1 • Lesson 2: Describing People

23

Exercises

I: Listen to the story and choose the correct answer.
Visit **basicesl.com/workbook-1/lesson-02** to listen to the story.

1. Mary is the ___niece___ of Paul.

   a. niece (circled)   **b.** nephew   **c.** aunt

2. Mary is _____ and beautiful.

   a. ugly   **b.** young   **c.** shy

3. Peter and Mary are _____ .

   a. cousins   **b.** married   **c.** single

4. John is the _____ of Paul.

   a. niece   **b.** son   **c.** nephew

5. John is _____ .

   a. married   **b.** single   **c.** sad

6. Sara and Ann are _____ .

   a. sisters   **b.** cousins   **c.** brothers

7. Sara is _____ .

   a. polite   **b.** rude   **c.** shy

8. Ann is _____ .

   a. polite   **b.** rude   **c.** shy

Lesson 3

Age
Possessive adjectives
Contractions with the verb *to be*
Asking for age

 basicesl.com/workbook-1/lesson-03

- ☐ Watch vocabulary video. Listen and repeat.
- ☐ Complete vocabulary exercises. (**Download**)
- ☐ Watch grammar video. Listen and repeat.
- ☐ Complete grammar exercises. (**Workbook**)
- ☐ Complete extra grammar exercises. (**Download**)
- ☐ Take a quiz. (**Download**)

Vocabulary

1. baby
2. child
3. teenager
4. adult
5. man
6. woman
7. boy
8. girl
9. party
10. cake
11. food
12. drink
13. birthday
14. wedding
15. gift
16. card
17. big (*adj*)
18. small (*adj*)
19. fun (*adj*)
20. boring (*adj*)

21. age (*noun*)
22. year (*noun*)
23. guest (*noun*)
24. here (*noun*)
25. calm (*adj*)
26. excited (*adj*)
27. sorry (*adj*)
28. angry (*adj*)
29. with (*prep*)

basicesl.com/workbook-1/lesson-03

Grammar

Possessive adjectives

Question	Answer
What is **my** party like?	**Your** party is fun.
What is **your** cake like?	**My** cake is big.
What is the son of Tom like?	**His** son is calm.
What is the baby of Mary like?	**Her** baby is beautiful.
What is the party like?	**Its** guests are excited.
What are **your** parents like?	**Our** parents are old.
What are **our** teenagers like?	**Your** teenagers are angry.
What are **their** in-laws like?	**Their** in-laws are mean.

Possessive adjectives show relationships or possession between people and things.

I → **my**	we → **our**
you → **your**	you → **your**
he → **his**	they → **their**
she → **her**	
it → **its**	

Contractions with the verb *to be*

Statement	pronoun + *to be*	
I **am** a father.	**I'm** a father.	
You **are** a mother.	**You're** a mother.	
He **is** my child.	**He's** my child.	
She **is** your baby.	**She's** your baby.	
It **is** my birthday.	**It's** my birthday.	
We **are** adults.	**We're** adults.	
They **are** guests.	**They're** guests.	

Negative statement	pronoun + *to be*	*to be* + not
I **am not** a father.	**I'm** not a father.	--
You **are not** a mother.	**You're** not a mother.	You **aren't** a mother.
He **is not** my child.	**He's** not my child.	He **isn't** my child.
She **is not** your baby.	**She's** not your baby.	She **isn't** your baby.
It **is not** my birthday.	**It's** not my birthday.	It **isn't** my birthday.
We **are not** adults.	**We're** not adults.	We **aren't** adults.
They **are not** guests.	**They're** not guests.	They **aren't** guests.

Contractions in statements with the verb *to be* are made with subject pronouns and the words *am*, *is* and *are*.

am → **'m**	**I'm**
is → **'s**	**he's, she's, it's**
are → **'re**	**we're, they're**

Contractions in negative statements are made two ways. One way is with the subject pronoun and the verb *to be*.

Another way is with the verb *to be* and the word *not*. There is no contraction for *am* and *not*.

is not → **isn't**
are not → **aren't**

Asking for age

Question	Answer
How old *is* your baby?	My baby *is* **one year old**.
How old *is* their child?	Their child *is* **eight years old**.
How old *are* the girls?	They *are* **sixteen years old**.
How old *are* the guests?	The guests *are* **thirty years old**.

How old is Tony?
He is **twelve years old**. He is not eleven years old.

How old are you and Tim?
We are **forty years old**. We are not thirty years old.

How old are you?
I am **fifty years old**. I am not sixty years old.

To ask for the age of a noun, use the question word *how*, the adjective *old* and the verb *to be*.

How old + *to be* + subject ?

Numbers are used as adjectives to describe nouns. A number before the words *years old* is used to describe age.

Subject + *to be* + **age**.
age = **number** + *year(s) old*

Workbook 1 • Lesson 3: Age

Exercises

A: Use the correct possessive adjective for the given subject: **my, your, his, her, its, our, their**.

1. (**I**) __My__ cake is big.
2. (**You**) _____ gift is small.
3. (**We**) _____ party is fun.
4. (**He**) _____ brother is mean.
5. (**She**) _____ sister is pretty.
6. (**It**) _____ guests are excited.
7. (**They**) _____ grandparents are old.
8. (**You**) _____ child is young.
9. (**We**) _____ cake is big.
10. (**They**) _____ boy is big.
11. (**He**) _____ wife is beautiful.
12. (**I**) _____ father is tall.
13. (**You**) _____ parents are nice.
14. (**She**) _____ husband is handsome.

B: Complete the sentence with the present tense form of the verb to be: **am, is, are**. (Review)

1. Ann __is__ my sister-in-law.
2. I _____ the mother of Amanda.
3. Steve and Sheila _____ married.
4. Mark and I _____ cousins.
5. William _____ my guest.
6. Olivia _____ a nice name.
7. I _____ the grandfather of Rodney.
8. You _____ rude and mean.
9. He _____ polite and nice.
10. Ann _____ funny and smart.
11. Mexico _____ big.
12. My brother _____ honest.
13. We _____ honest.
14. They _____ angry.

C: Write the **opposite** adjective. (Review)

1. mean __nice__
2. handsome _____
3. young _____
4. fat _____
5. polite _____
6. ugly _____
7. sad _____
8. bad _____
9. short _____
10. confident _____

basicesl.com/workbook-1/lesson-03

Exercises

D: Write the statement using a **contraction.**

1. **She is** twelve years old.   *She's twelve years old.*
2. **I am** with the guests.   _____
3. **They are** excited.   _____
4. **We are** brothers.   _____
5. **You are** an aunt.   _____
6. **He is** with my uncle.   _____
7. **It is** my birthday.   _____
8. **She is** my mother.   _____
9. **He is** confident and handsome.   _____
10. **I am** sorry.   _____

E: Write the negative statement using a **contraction.**

1. **We are** not young.   *We're not young.*
2. He **is not** old.   _____
3. **It is** not fun.   _____
4. They **are not** with her family.   _____
5. **You are** not my brother.   _____
6. Tim and I **are not** shy.   _____
7. It **is not** her birthday.   _____
8. Jane and Mary **are not** happy.   _____
9. We **are not** angry.   _____
10. **I am** not with Jerry.   _____

Workbook 1 • Lesson 3: Age

Exercises

F: Make the sentence **negative**. Use <u>contractions</u> with the verb *to be*. Follow the example.

1. She is five years old.

    no contraction   ***She is not** five years old.*

    pronoun + *to be*   ***She's not** five years old.*

    to be + not   ***She <u>isn't</u>** five years old.*

2. You are eleven years old.

    no contraction   _____

    pronoun + *to be*   _____

    to be + not   _____

3. They are big gifts.

    no contraction   _____

    pronoun + *to be*   _____

    to be + not   _____

4. It is with my family.

    no contraction   _____

    pronoun + *to be*   _____

    to be + not   _____

5. We are twelve years old.

    no contraction   _____

    pronoun + *to be*   _____

    to be + not   _____

6. I am fifty years old.

    no contraction   _____

    pronoun + *to be*   _____

basicesl.com/workbook-1/lesson-03

Exercises

G: Form one question and two statements with the given clues. Follow the example.

1. Mary

*What is **Mary** like?*
*She **isn't** old.*
***She's** young.*

2. John and Jose

3. cake

4. Gina and I

5. you and Sara

6. you

Workbook 1 • Lesson 3: Age

Exercises

H: Change **Ann** *(girl)* to **Tom** *(boy)* and rewrite the story. Use **contractions** for the underlined words.

Ann is my friend. <u>She is</u> thirteen years old. She is a teenager. She <u>is not</u> an adult.

Her birthday party is fun. It <u>is not</u> boring. Her cake is big. <u>It is</u> not small.

<u>I am</u> with Ann and her cousins. Her cousins are Jane and Lee. <u>They are</u> nice. They <u>are not</u> mean.

The guests of Ann are happy and excited. Her guests <u>are not</u> mean and rude.

Tom is my friend. **He's**...

I: Listen to the story and choose the correct answer.
Visit **basicesl.com/workbook-1/lesson-03** to listen to the story.

1. Tom is ___*fifteen*___ years old.   a. twelve   b. nine   **c. fifteen** (circled)
2. The family of Tom is from _____ .   a. India   b. Mexico   c. China
3. Tom is with his mother, father and _____ .   a. brothers   b. sisters   c. cousins
4. Tony is _____ years old.   a. eight   b. twelve   c. fourteen
5. John is _____ years old.   a. eight   b. twelve   c. fourteen
6. Tom and his family are _____ .   a. fun   b. boring   c. rude
7. The grandmother isn't _____ .   a. shy   b. nice   c. mean
8. The grandfather is _____ .   a. smart   b. skinny   c. funny

Lesson 4

School
Simple present statements
Asking for location

 basicesl.com/workbook-1/lesson-04

- [ ] Watch vocabulary video. Listen and repeat.
- [ ] Complete vocabulary exercises. (**Download**)
- [ ] Watch grammar video. Listen and repeat.
- [ ] Complete grammar exercises. (**Workbook**)
- [ ] Complete extra grammar exercises. (**Download**)
- [ ] Take a quiz. (**Download**)

Vocabulary

21. to love (*verb*)
22. to like (*verb*)
23. to play (*verb*)
24. to learn (*verb*)
25. to teach (*verb**)
26. to laugh (*verb*)
27. to talk (*verb*)
28. to listen (*verb*)
29. to hug (*verb*)

*Irregular verb list page 6

Grammar

Simple present statements

to like	Singular	Plural
1st	I like Tom.	We like cake.
2nd	You like Mary.	You like gifts.
3rd	He **likes** Sarah. She **likes** Sean. It **likes** John.	They like school.

For most verbs, the simple present tense form is the same for all subjects, except **3rd person singular** subjects.

3rd person singular

he → Adam
she → Anna
it → Africa

For 3rd person singular subjects (*he*, *she*, and *it*), add an **-s** to the base form of the verb.

Singular	Plural
I love	We love
You love	You love
He **loves**	They love
She **loves**	
It **loves**	

to love
I love my teacher.
You love your teacher.

He **loves** his teacher.
She **loves** her teacher.
It **loves** the teacher.

We love our teacher.
You love your teacher.
They love their teacher.

to sit
I sit in my classroom.
You sit in your classroom.

He **sits** in his classroom.
She **sits** in her classroom.
It **sits** in the classroom.

We sit in our classroom.
You sit in your classroom.
They sit in their classroom.

to walk
I walk with my teacher.
You walk with your teacher.

He **walks** with his teacher.
She **walks** with her teacher.
It **walks** with the teacher.

We walk with our teacher.
You walk with your teacher.
They walk with their teacher.

to listen
I listen to my coach.
You listen to your coach.

He **listens** to his coach.
She **listens** to her coach.
It **listens** to the coach.

We listen to our coach.
You listen to your coach.
They listen to their coach.

Asking for location

Question	Answer
Where *am* I?	You *are* **on the playground.**
Where *are* you?	I *am* **at the library.**
Where *is* the principal?	She *is* **in her office.**
Where *is* the restroom?	It's **in the cafeteria.**
Where *are* you and Jim?	We're **at our school.**
Where *are* the girls?	They're **in the gym.**

To ask for location use the question word *where* with the verb *to be*.

The words *in*, *at*, and *on* are common prepositions used to answer *where* questions.

Workbook 1 • Lesson 4: School

Exercises

A: Complete the sentence in the simple present tense with the verb *to love*.

1. I __love__ Emily.
2. You _____ the playground.
3. He _____ Mary.
4. She _____ her school.
5. We _____ our parents.
6. They _____ their parents.
7. Tony _____ his daughter.
8. The girls _____ their cousins.
9. My brother _____ her.
10. Their family _____ Tony.
11. Our family _____ Tony.
12. Sue and Liz _____ my son.

B: Complete the sentence with the correct **possessive adjective** for the **subject** in bold. (Review)

1. **John** loves __his__ sisters.
2. A **grandson** loves _____ grandmother.
3. My **teacher** loves _____ students.
4. **You** love _____ father.
5. **I** love _____ mother.
6. **They** love _____ son and daughter.
7. **We** love _____ mother and father.
8. **Mary and Lucy** love _____ brother.
9. **Mary and I** love _____ sister.
10. **You and Mary** love _____ school.
11. **We** love _____ big classroom.
12. **Ann** loves _____ teacher.

C: Answer the *where* question with the given **location**. Use a <u>contraction</u> (subject pronoun +*to be*).

1. **classroom** Where is the Mr. Nick? __He's in the **classroom**.__
2. **restroom** Where are the girls? _____
3. **library** Where are you? _____
4. **office** Where is the Mrs. Nancy? _____
5. **cafeteria** Where am I? _____
6. **school** Where is the restroom? _____

basicesl.com/workbook-1/lesson-04

Exercises

D: Complete the simple present tense sentence with the correct form of the verb.

1. **to sit** He _sits_ with the coach.
2. **to stand** They _stand_ with Alex.
3. **to talk** The son _____ to his parents.
4. **to love** Pam _____ her mother.
5. **to learn** I _____ in my classroom.
6. **to laugh** He _____ on the playground.
7. **to stand** The son _____ with Susan.
8. **to love** You _____ your daughter.
9. **to learn** I _____ with my friends.
10. **to laugh** They _____ at the office.
11. **to play** You _____ on the playground.
12. **to play** Tom _____ in the gym.
13. **to sit** We _____ in the classroom.
14. **to like** Tom and I _____ our school.
15. **to hug** Tom _____ his mother.
16. **to like** She _____ school.
17. **to run** She _____ to the playground.
18. **to run** I _____ on the playground.
19. **to talk** You and Tom _____ .
20. **to talk** They _____ to the principal.

E: Change **Kathryn** to **Kathryn and Holly** and rewrite the story. Use <u>contractions</u>.

Kathryn is a student. She is smart and polite. <u>She is</u> sixteen years old. She <u>is not</u> from the United States. <u>She is</u> from France.

Kathryn learns English at her school. Her teacher is Mrs. Gonzalez. Kathryn sits with her friends in the classroom. She listens to her teacher.

Kathryn and Holly...

Workbook 1 • Lesson 4: School

Exercises

F: Follow the example.

1. coach / **to run**

Where is the coach?

He's (She's) in the gym.

*The coach **runs** in the gym.*

2. boys / **to learn**

3. we / **to laugh**

4. students / **to sit**

5. Mark / **to talk**

6. you / **to teach**

basicesl.com/workbook-1/lesson-04

Exercises

G: Answer the question in the **simple present tense**. Use the given clues. Follow the example.

1. Where is Mary?

   classroom — *Mary is in the classroom.*

   to learn / classmates — *She learns **with** her classmates.*

2. Where are we?

   library — _____

   to sit / teacher — _____

3. Where is the coach?

   gym — _____

   to run / students — _____

4. Where are the girls?

   playground — _____

   to play / friends — _____

5. Where are the students?

   office — _____

   to talk / principal — _____

Workbook 1 • Lesson 4: School

Exercises

H: Listen to the story and choose the correct answer.
Visit **basicesl.com/workbook-1/lesson-04** to listen to the story.

1. Dan __loves_____ his school.

                                a. laughs   **b.** likes   **(c.)** loves

2. His school is _____ .

                                a. big   **b.** new   **c.** old

3. His teacher is _____ .

                                a. smart   **b.** shy   **c.** nice

4. Amy learns in the _____.

                                a. library   **b.** classroom   **c.** office

5. Dan and Amy sit in the _____ .

                                a. library   **b.** cafeteria   **c.** classroom

6. The playground is _____.

                                a. fun   **b.** boring   **c.** nice

7. The _____ run and laugh on the playground.

                                a. classmates   **b.** students   **c.** boys

8. Their teachers _____ in the office.

                                a. stand   **b.** play   **c.** sit

basicesl.com/workbook-1/lesson-04

Lesson 5

Classroom
Simple present negative statements
Math statements

 basicesl.com/workbook-1/lesson-05

- ☐ Watch vocabulary video. Listen and repeat.
- ☐ Complete vocabulary exercises. (**Download**)
- ☐ Watch grammar video. Listen and repeat.
- ☐ Complete grammar exercises. (**Workbook**)
- ☐ Complete extra grammar exercises. (**Download**)
- ☐ Take a quiz. (**Download**)

Vocabulary

21. easy (*adj*)
22. difficult (*adj*)
23. to study (*verb*)
24. to show (*verb*)
25. to correct (*verb*)
26. to know (*verb**)
27. to remember (*verb*)
28. to forget (*verb**)
29. to understand (*verb**)

* *Irregular verb list page 6*

Grammar

Simple present negative statements

In simple present statements, most verbs add *-s* for 3rd person singular subjects. Negative statements use the base form of the main verb for all subjects.

Statement	Negative statement
I know math.	I **do not** know math.
You study science.	You **do not** study science.
He *remembers* the answer.	He **does not** *remember* the answer.
She *plays* music.	She **does not** *play* music.
It *understands* language.	It **does not** *understand* language.
We read the lessons.	We **do not** read the lessons.
They answer the questions.	They **do not** answer the questions.

Contractions are common in the English language. The contractions *don't* or *doesn't* are used in present tense negative statements.

Negative statement	Negative statement with contraction
I **do not** know.	I **don't** know.
You **do not** study.	You **don't** study.
He **does not** remember.	He **doesn't** remember.
She **does not** play.	She **doesn't** play.
It **does not** understand.	It **doesn't** understand.
We **do not** read.	We **don't** read.
They **do not** answer.	They **don't** answer.

Simple present tense negative statements use the helping verbs *do* or *does*. The word *does* is used in 3rd person singular statements.

Singular	Plural
I do	We do
You do	You do
He **does**	They do
She **does**	
It **does**	

In negative statements the helping verb *do* or *does* is followed by the word *not* and the base form of the main verb.

subject + **do not** + verb
subject + **does not** + verb

Contractions are made with the helping verb *do* or *does* and the word *not*.

do not → **don't**
does not → **doesn't**

Basic math

Below are examples of basic math equations.

addition	*to add*	plus (+)
2 + 2 = 4	Two **plus** two **equals** four.	
subtraction	*to subtract*	minus (-)
2 - 0 = 2	Two **minus** zero **equals** two.	
multiplication	*to multiply*	times (×)
2 × 3 = 6	Two **times** three **equals** six.	
division	*to divide*	divided by (÷)
10 ÷ 2 = 5	Ten **divided by** two **equals** five.	

The basic math operations are represented with symbols:

+ **plus**
- **minus**
× **times (multiplied by)**
÷ **divided by**
= **equals**

Workbook 1 • Lesson 5: Classroom

Exercises

A: Complete the negative statement with **do** or **does**.

1. I __do__ not know French.
2. She _____ not enjoy music.
3. Nancy _____ not read English.
4. You _____ not understand.
5. The student _____ not like geography.
6. The students _____ not study math.
7. He _____ not write the exercises.
8. We _____ not talk in the library.
9. Mary and I _____ not play in class.
10. You and Mary _____ not sit.
11. It _____ not walk.
12. They _____ not remember.

B: Change the statement to a **negative statement**. Do not use contractions.

1. I love math.   _I **do not** love math._
2. You read French.   _____
3. He understands science.   _____
4. She knows the answer.   _____
5. Jim ask questions.   _____
6. It plays music.   _____
7. We like art.   _____
8. They study history.   _____

C: Complete the **negative** statement. Use contractions.

1. I __don't__ understand Chinese.
2. We _____ like music.
3. Julia _____ ask easy questions.
4. John _____ answer difficult questions.
5. The student _____ love math.
6. The students _____ love art.
7. He _____ read at the school.
8. Tom and I _____ sit in the cafeteria.
9. Cecilia _____ come to class.
10. It _____ play music.
11. We _____ like wrong answers.
12. They _____ know their history.

basicesl.com/workbook-1/lesson-05

Exercises

D: Make the statements **negative**. Do not use contractions. Follow the example.

1. Lucy **writes** in English. Her English teacher **is** good.

*Lucy **does not write** in English. Her English teacher **is not** good.*

2. Tim likes math and science. Math is easy.

_____

3. Ray reads in the classroom. The teacher is serious.

_____

4. She loves music. Music is fun.

_____

5. We study in the library. The librarian is nice.

_____

6. The girls love art. It is easy.

_____

E: Write out the math equation. Follow the example.

1. $3 + 3 = 6$ *Three plus three equals six.*

2. $4 \times 2 = 6$ _____

3. $5 - 0 = 5$ _____

4. $6 \div 2 = 3$ _____

5. $12 - 1 = 11$ _____

6. $2 \times 10 = 20$ _____

7. $13 - 4 = 9$ _____

8. $15 \div 3 = 5$ _____

Workbook 1 • Lesson 5: Classroom

Exercises

F: Form sentences with the given clues. Follow the example. Use contractions.

1. Kathy (**12**) / **to like** / art

   How old is Kathy?
   *She's **twelve** years old.*
   *Kathy **likes** history.*
   *She **doesn't like** art.*

2. girls (**9**) / **to study** / health

3. boy (**11**) / **to love** / tests

4. Pam (**7**) / **to write** / question

5. Tom (**8**) / **to know** / music

basicesl.com/workbook-1/lesson-05

Exercises

G: Rewrite the story and make **each sentence negative**. Do **not** use contractions.

Pam **is** my friend. She **is** twelve years old. She **likes** art and history. She **reads** history with her teacher.

Pam **loves** her teacher. Mrs. Brown **is** from England. She **is** twenty-five years old.

Pam **is** smart. She **writes** in her English class. She **asks** questions in her classroom. She **learns** Spanish at school.

Lucy **is** a friend of Pam. She **likes** math and science. Pam and Lucy **sit** together on the playground.

*Pam **is not** my ...*

Workbook 1 • Lesson 5: Classroom

Exercises

H: Listen to the story and choose the correct answer.
Visit **basicesl.com/workbook-1/lesson-05** to listen to the story.

1. Ray is __*fifteen*__ years old.   **a.** fifteen   **b.** sixteen   **c.** seventeen

2. Ray likes _____ and music.   **a.** math   **b.** art   **c.** geography

3. Ray doesn't like _____ .   **a.** math   **b.** art   **c.** geography

4. Math is _____ for Ray to understand.
   a. easy   **b.** difficult   **c.** boring

5. Pam loves math and _____ .   **a.** history   **b.** music   **c.** science

6. Pam doesn't _____ art.   **a.** write   **b.** understand   **c.** learn

7. The family of Pam is from _____ .
   a. Mexico   **b.** China   **c.** France

8. The family of Pam speaks _____ .
   a. Spanish   **b.** Chinese   **c.** French

9. Pam is _____ years old.   **a.** fifteen   **b.** sixteen   **c.** seventeen

10. Lucy isn't very _____ .   **a.** fun   **b.** nice   **c.** confident

11. Lucy doesn't like _____ class.   **a.** history   **b.** math   **c.** science

12. Lucy learns _____ .   **a.** Spanish   **b.** Chinese   **c.** English

Lesson 6

School Supplies

Simple present statements with *to be*, *to have*, *to go* and *to do*
Using the helping verb *to do* for emphasis

 basicesl.com/workbook-1/lesson-06

- ☐ Watch vocabulary video. Listen and repeat.
- ☐ Complete vocabulary exercises. (**Download**)
- ☐ Watch grammar video. Listen and repeat.
- ☐ Complete grammar exercises. (**Workbook**)
- ☐ Complete extra grammar exercises. (**Download**)
- ☐ Take a quiz. (**Download**)

Vocabulary

1. desk	**2.** chair	**3.** whiteboard	**4.** marker
5. book	**6.** notebook	**7.** pen	**8.** pencil
9. computer	**10.** backpack	**11.** ruler	**12.** eraser
13. map	**14.** flag	**15.** scissors	**16.** glue
17. wastebasket	**18.** clock	**19.** calculator	**20.** paper

21. mistake (*noun*) **22.** grade (*noun*) **23.** to erase (*verb*)

24. to want (*verb*) **25.** to use (*verb*) **26.** to type (*verb*)

27. to have (*verb**) **28.** to do (*verb**) **29.** to go (*verb**)

* *Irregular verb list page 6*

basicesl.com/workbook-1/lesson-06

Grammar

Simple present statements with *to be*, *to have*, *to go* and *to do*

to be	Singular	Plural
1st	I **am** a happy teacher.	We **are** happy teachers.
2nd	You **are** an honest boy.	You **are** smart boys.
3rd	He **is** a good student. She **is** a good student. It **is** a good pen.	They **are** good students.

to have	Singular	Plural
1st	I **have** a flag.	We **have** maps.
2nd	You **have** a backpack.	You **have** the markers.
3rd	He **has** a computer. She **has** a ruler. It **has** an eraser.	They **have** pens.

to go	Singular	Plural
1st	I **go** to the gym.	We **go** to class.
2nd	You **go** to the library.	You **go** to the library.
3rd	He **goes** to the office. She **goes** to the cafeteria. It **goes** on the desk.	They **go** to the playground.

to do	Singular	Plural
1st	I **do** not have scissors.	We **do** not have chairs.
2nd	You **do** not go to class.	You **do** not go to the gym.
3rd	He **does** not have a pen. She **does** not have glue. It **does** not have paper.	They **do** not have notebooks.

Some verbs have different forms or different spelling rules in the present tense.

The verb *to be* has three different forms in the present tense.

to be → **am, are, is**

The verb *to have* has two forms in the present tense. The word *has* is used for **3rd person singular** subjects.

to have → **have, has**

The verb *to go* has two forms in the present tense. The word *goes* is used for **3rd person singular** subjects.

to go → **go, goes**

The verb *to do* has two forms in the present tense. The word *does* is used for **3rd person singular** subjects.

to do → **do, does**

Using the helping verb *to do* for emphasis

Statement	Statement with emphasis
I want my calculator.	I **do** want my calculator.
You have a computer.	You **do** have a computer.
He erases his mistakes.	He **does** erase his mistakes.
She uses her scissors.	She **does** use her scissors.
It has a map.	It **does** have a map.
We want our pencils.	We **do** want our pencils.
They answer the questions.	They **do** answer the questions.

The helping verb *to do* is used to make negative statements. The helping verb *to do* is also used in affirmative statements to add emphasis.

do + verb
does + verb

Exercises

A: Complete the simple present sentence with the verb *to have*.

1. I _have_ three pencils.
2. She _____ one pencil.
3. She doesn't _____ a pen.
4. Our teacher _____ good students.
5. Their classroom _____ a French student.
6. We _____ Chinese students in our class.
7. The lesson _____ ten exercises.
8. You and I don't _____ a calculator.
9. John _____ a computer in his backpack.
10. He _____ books in his backpack.
11. The classroom doesn't _____ a clock.
12. My desk doesn't _____ a chair.

B: Complete the simple present sentence with the verb *to go*.

1. I _go_ to school with Lucy.
2. He _____ to the gymnasium.
3. He doesn't _____ to school with Lucy.
4. John _____ to school with Ann.
5. You _____ to school with your brother.
6. You and John _____ with the teacher.
7. My friends don't _____ to art class.
8. The girl _____ to learn music.
9. The boy doesn't _____ with her.
10. The flag _____ with the map.
11. The flags _____ in the classroom.
12. The flag doesn't _____ in the restroom.

C: Rewrite the statement **with emphasis** and as a **negative statement**. Use contractions.

1. The question shows an answer.   *The question **does** show an answer.*
   *The question **doesn't** show an answer.*

2. I want my ruler.   _____

3. She has two notebooks.   _____

4. It corrects the tests.   _____

basicesl.com/workbook-1/lesson-06

Exercises

D: Rewrite the statement with the new **subject pronoun**. Follow the example.

1. **They** go to the classroom. **(she)**   *She **goes** to the classroom.*

2. **They** learn in the classroom. **(he)** _____

3. **We** have three pens. **(John)** _____

4. **Sarah** has a ruler. **(I)** _____

5. **Tom** is in the cafeteria. **(we)** _____

6. **You** aren't at your desk. **(I)** _____

7. **Science class** isn't difficult. **(they)** _____

8. **I** am not happy. **(You and Mary)** _____

9. **Tom** isn't in the cafeteria. **(we)** _____

10. **The principal** wants a chair. **(I)** _____

11. **The lessons** don't have mistakes. **(it)** _____

12. **Tom and I** don't use glue. **(Tom)** _____

13. **She** doesn't correct the papers. **(I)** _____

14. **They** don't like history class. **(he)** _____

15. **We** don't remember our grades. **(she)** _____

16. **They** do speak Chinese. **(Jimmy)** _____

17. **Jose** does know French. **(I)** _____

18. **I** do have five books. **(Sarah)** _____

19. **Mr. Smith** does have a marker. **(you)** _____

20. **It** does have paper. **(you)** _____

Exercises

E: Write sentences with the given clues. Follow the example.

1. Mike / to have / pencil (**3**)

*Mike **doesn't** have a pen.*

*He **does** have pencils.*

*He has **three** pencils.*

2. girls / to have / ruler (**4**)

3. student / to go / class (**1**)

4. boys / to play / playground (**2**)

5. I / to understand / lesson (**5**)

basicesl.com/workbook-1/lesson-06

Exercises

F: Change *I* to *she* and rewrite the story. Use contractions.

I **like** my school. I **go** to school with my friends. I **have** two good friends. My friends are Josh and Ashley. I **have** one class with Josh. I don't **have** a class with Ashley.

I don't **go** to the playground with Ashley. I do **go** to the playground with Josh.

I **understand** my history lesson. I don't **understand** my math lesson. I don't **use** my geography book. I do **use** my science book.

She likes her ...

Exercises

G: Write out the math statement. Follow the example. (Review)

1. 8 + 13 = 21   *Eight plus thirteen equals twenty-one.*
2. 3 x 0 = 0   _____
3. 14 x 1 = 14   _____
4. 18 / 2 = 9   _____
5. 15 - 7 = 8   _____
6. 12 / 1 = 12   _____
7. 29 - 28 = 1   _____
8. 15 + 12 = 27   _____

H. Listen to the story and choose the correct answer.
Visit **basicesl.com/workbook-1/lesson-06** to listen to the story.

1. Greg is the ___cousin___ of Alan.   **a.** cousin   **b.** brother   **c.** father
2. Greg likes _____ .   **a.** science   **b.** art   **c.** geography
3. Greg does not like _____ .   **a.** math   **b.** music   **c.** history
4. Greg has two _____ and a notebook.   **a.** rulers   **b.** erasers   **c.** pencils
5. Greg does not have a _____ at school.   **a.** computer   **b.** calculator   **c.** scissors
6. Greg _____ scissors and glue.   **a.** does have   **b.** doesn't have
7. Greg goes to the _____ in the morning.   **a.** auditorium   **b.** library   **c.** gym
8. Greg _____ in the library.   **a.** does study   **b.** doesn't study   **c.** reads
8. Greg _____ in the library.   **a.** talks   **b.** reads   **c.** plays
9. Greg remembers the map from _____ .   **a.** geography   **b.** history   **c.** science

basicesl.com/workbook-1/lesson-06

Lesson 7

House
Questions with the verb *to be*
Using question words with the verb *to be*

 basicesl.com/workbook-1/lesson-07

- ☐ Watch vocabulary video. Listen and repeat.
- ☐ Complete vocabulary exercises. (**Download**)
- ☐ Watch grammar video. Listen and repeat.
- ☐ Complete grammar exercises. (**Workbook**)
- ☐ Complete extra grammar exercises. (**Download**)
- ☐ Take a quiz. (**Download**)

Vocabulary

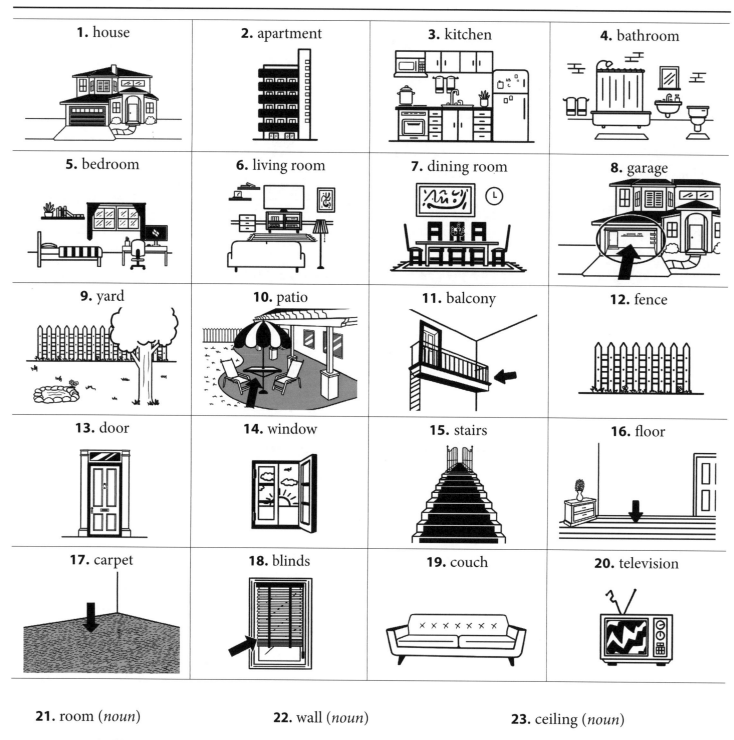

21. room (*noun*)
22. wall (*noun*)
23. ceiling (*noun*)
24. open (*adj*)
25. closed (*adj*)
26. clean (*adj*)
27. dirty (*adj*)
28. upstairs (*adv*)
29. downstairs (*adv*)

basicesl.com/workbook-1/lesson-07

Grammar

Questions with the verb *to be*

Statement	Question
I **am** in the bedroom.	**Am** I in the bedroom?
You **are** on the stairs.	**Are** you on the stairs?
He **is** on the roof.	**Is** he on the roof?
She **is** at her house.	**Is** she at her house?
It **is** in the living room.	**Is** it in the living room?
We **are** at the door.	**Are** we at the door?
They **are** on the couch.	**Are** they on the couch?

Question	Answer
Is the bathroom upstairs?	**Yes,** it **is** upstairs.
	No, it **is not** upstairs.
Is she in the garage?	**Yes,** she **is** in the garage.
	No, she's not in the garage.
Are you at the apartment?	**Yes,** I **am** at the apartment.
	No, I'm not at the apartment.
Are they on the balcony?	**Yes,** they **are** on the balcony.
	No, they **aren't** on the balcony.
Are the bedrooms dirty?	**Yes,** they **are.**
	No, they **aren't.**
Is the window open?	**Yes,** it **is.**
	No, it's not.

Present tense questions with the verb *to be* begin with **am**, **is** or **are**. The verb *to be* is followed by the subject. The form of the verb *to be* depends on the subject.

Singular	Plural
Am I	**Are** we
Are you	**Are** you
Is he	**Are** they
Is she	
Is it	

We use *yes* and *no* to answer questions with the verb *to be*. *Yes* and *no* are followed by a comma and a statement. A *no* answer is followed by a negative statement.

Yes, + statement
No, + negative statement

A short answer is formed with only the subject and the verb *to be*. Only use contractions in negative short answers.

Using question words with the verb *to be*

Question	Answer
Is Mark in the kitchen?	No, he's not in the kitchen.
Who is in the kitchen?	**Steve** is in the kitchen.
Is your name John?	No, my name is not John.
What is your name?	My name is **Jake**.
Is it your birthday?	No, it's not.
When is your birthday?	My birthday is **on Friday**.
Is the bathroom upstairs?	No, it isn't upstairs.
Where is the bathroom?	It is **downstairs**.

Use the question words *who*, *what*, *when*, and *where* before the verb *to be* to ask for information.

Who ... ?	People
What ... ?	Information
When ... ?	Time
Where ... ?	Location

Workbook 1 • Lesson 7: House

Exercises

A: Change the statement to a **question**.

1. Mary is in the kitchen. — *Is Mary in the kitchen?*
2. The windows are open. _____
3. The balcony is big. _____
4. You are on the balcony. _____
5. The desks are in the classrooms. _____
6. Henry is in the garage. _____
7. The girls are in the restroom. _____
8. The fence is nice. _____
9. The doors are old. _____
10. The carpet is dirty. _____
11. The parents are angry. _____
12. The coach is serious. _____

B: Use the clue to complete the question with *who*, *what*, *when*, *where*, or *how*.

1. Q: _Where_ is Lamar? A: He is **in the bathroom**.
2. Q: _____ is Lamar? A: He is **my cousin**.
3. Q: _____ old is Lamar? A: Lamar is **twenty-eight years** old.
4. Q: _____ is Lamar like? A: He is **funny**.
5. Q: _____ is his sister like? A: She is **very nice**.
6. Q: _____ is your father home? A: He is home **at night**.
7. Q: _____ are they? A: They are **our teachers**.
8. Q: _____ are the bedrooms? A: They are **upstairs**.

Exercises

C: Answer the question with a **yes (Y)** or **no (N)** statement. Write a long answer and short answer. Use contractions with the word **not**. Follow the example.

1. Is the window small? **(Y)** *Yes, the window **is** small.*
   *Yes, it **is**.*

2. Are the blinds open? **(N)** *No, the blinds **aren't** open.*
   *No, they **aren't**.*

3. Is the fence closed? **(N)**

4. Are the boys in the garage? **(Y)**

5. Am I at your apartment? **(N)**

6. Is the couch in the living room? **(Y)**

7. Are you downstairs? **(Y)**

8. Is the chair on the patio? **(N)**

9. Are the scissors in the kitchen? **(N)**

10. Is the bathroom dirty? **(Y)**

Exercises

D: Read the story and answer the questions. Use complete sentences and <u>contractions</u>. Follow the example.

Ruby: I am at my house in the kitchen. Where are you?

Frank: I am at my apartment on the balcony. I am with my brother and sister. They are in the living room on the couch. They talk and study in the living room. Who is at your house?

Ruby: My family is at my house. My mother is on the patio. She likes to read on the patio. My father is in the dining room. He has a computer. My brother is upstairs with his books. What is your apartment like?

Frank: My apartment is small. My bedroom is nice and clean. Is your house small?

Ruby: No, it isn't. My house is big. It has four bedrooms and three bathrooms. The kitchen is clean and nice. We have art on the wall in the dining room.

Frank: My sister Lisa likes art. She has an art class at school. She reads books about art in her history class at school.

1. <u>Where</u> is Ruby?

   <u>She's at her house in the kitchen</u>.

2. Where is Frank?

   _____

3. Who is Frank with?

   _____

4. What is Frank's bedroom like?

   _____

5. Where is the art at Ruby's house?

   _____

6. What does Lisa read in her history class?

   _____

Exercises

E: Follow the example.

1. Tom and Alex / <u>living room</u>

   Are Tom and Alex in the dining room?
   *No, they **aren't** in the dining room.*
   Where are they?
   ***They're** in the <u>living room</u>.*

2. Cynthia / house

3. You / office

4. Fred / bathroom

5. television / living room

Workbook 1 • Lesson 7: House

Exercises

F: Use question words (**who, what, how, when** and **where**) to form questions for the given answer.

1. Q: <u>_What_ is her name?</u>　　　　　　　　　　　　　　 A: Her name is **Betty**.
2. Q: _____　　　　 A: Betty is **forty-seven years old**.
3. Q: _____　　　　 A: **Raymond** is fifty-two years old.
4. Q: _____　　　　 A: He's **nice and funny**.
5. Q: _____　　　　 A: She's **on the balcony**.
6. Q: _____　　　　 A: Raymond is at the apartment **on Sunday**.
7. Q: _____　　　　 A: The couch is **in the living room**.
8. Q: _____　　　　 A: **Raymond** is the brother of Betty.

G: Listen to the story and choose the correct answer.
Visit **basicesl.com/workbook-1/lesson-07** to listen to the story.

1. Karen lives in a __*big*__ house.　　　　　　 a. clean　　 b. small　　 **c. big** (circled)
2. The house is _____ .　　　　　　　　　 a. old　　　 b. nice　　　 c. new
3. The _____ are ugly.　　　　　　　　　 a. stairs　　 b. windows　 c. blinds
4. The house has three _____ upstairs.　 a. bedrooms　 b. doors　　 c. bathrooms
5. Karen's father _____ in the yard.　　 a. talks　　 b. walks　　 c. runs
6. Her mother reads on the _____ .　　　 a. balcony　 b. patio　　 c. floor
7. Karen's _____ wants a television for the patio.

　　　　　　　　　　　　　　　　　　　　　　　 a. mother　 b. father　　 c. brother
8. Karen's brothers play on the _____ .　 a. garage　 b. patio　　 c. fence

basicesl.com/workbook-1/lesson-07

Lesson 8

Kitchen
Simple present questions
Using question words with simple present questions

 basicesl.com/workbook-1/lesson-08

- [ ] Watch vocabulary video. Listen and repeat.
- [ ] Complete vocabulary exercises. (**Download**)
- [ ] Watch grammar video. Listen and repeat.
- [ ] Complete grammar exercises. (**Workbook**)
- [ ] Complete extra grammar exercises. (**Download**)
- [ ] Take a quiz. (**Download**)

Vocabulary

1. table	**2.** tablecloth	**3.** plate	**4.** bowl
5. fork	**6.** knife	**7.** spoon	**8.** napkin
9. glass	**10.** cup	**11.** pot	**12.** pan
13. refrigerator	**14.** stove	**15.** microwave	**16.** oven
17. sink	**18.** shelf	**19.** cupboard	**20.** counter

21. to grab (*verb*)   **22.** to move (*verb*)   **23.** to open (*verb*)

24. to close (*verb*)   **25.** to get (*verb**)   **26.** to put (*verb**)

27. to wash (*verb*)   **28.** to take (*verb**)   **29.** to need (*verb*)

* *Irregular verb list page 6*

basicesl.com/workbook-1/lesson-08

Grammar

Simple present questions

Statement	Question
I **get** a knife.	**Do** I **get** a knife?
You **need** a plate.	**Do** you **need** a plate?
He **wants** a fork.	**Does** he **want** a fork?
She **has** a spoon.	**Does** she **have** a spoon?
It **gets** dirty.	**Does** it **get** dirty?
We **wash** the bowls.	**Do** we **wash** the bowls?
They **use** napkins.	**Do** they **use** napkins?

Question	Answer
Do you **want** a glass?	**Yes,** I **want** a glass.
	No, I **don't want** a glass.
Does she **have** a cup?	**Yes,** she **has** a cup.
	No, she **doesn't have** a cup.
Does the cupboard **get** dirty?	**Yes,** it **gets** dirty.
	No, it **does not get** dirty.
Do they **wash** the pans?	**Yes,** they **wash** the pans.
	No, they **don't wash** the pans.
Does the pot **go** on the stove?	**Yes,** it **does.**
	No, it **doesn't.**
Do you **put** plates in the sink?	**Yes,** I **do.**
	No, I **don't.**

Simple present tense questions with verbs other than *to be* use the helping verb *do* or *does*. The question begins with the word *do* or *does*, followed by the subject. The word *does* is used for 3rd person singular subjects.

Singular	Plural
Do I	**Do** we
Do you	**Do** you
Does he	**Do** they
Does she	
Does it	

Simple present tense questions always use the **base** form of the main verb.

Do + subject + **base verb** ... ?
Does + subject + **base verb** ... ?

Use *yes* and *no* to answer questions. A *no* answer is followed by a negative statement.

A short answer is formed with the subject and the verb *to do*.

Using question words with simple present questions

Question	Answer
Does she need a cup?	No, she doesn't.
What does she need?	She needs **a glass.**
Do we clean the oven?	Yes, we clean the oven.
When do we clean the oven?	We clean it **on Monday.**
Do the cups go on the shelf?	No, they don't.
Where do the cups go?	They go **in the cupboard.**
Do I get a plate from Mark?	No, you do not.
Who do I get a plate from?	You get a plate from **Sarah.**
Does Jim wash the plates?	No, he doesn't.
Who *washes* the plates?	**Kelly** washes the plates.

Use the question words *who, what, when* and *where* to ask for specific information.

Who ... ?	People
What ... ?	Information
When ... ?	Time
Where ... ?	Location

In the last question example, without the helping verb *do* or *does*, we **do not** use the base form of the main verb. We use the 3rd person singular verb form with question words like *who* or *what*.

Workbook 1 • Lesson 8: Kitchen

Exercises

A: Complete the sentences. Follow the example.

1. Q: __Does__ Lucy **want** a glass?   A: No, she doesn't __want__ a glass.
2. Q: _____ he **have** a fork?   A: Yes, he _____ a fork.
3. Q: _____ they **get** more napkins?   A: No, they don't _____ more napkins.
4. Q: _____ she **go** to the sink?   A: Yes, she _____ to the sink.
5. Q: _____ I **put** it on the counter?   A: No, you don't _____ it on the counter.
6. Q: _____ the table **need** a tablecloth?   A: Yes, it _____ a tablecloth.

B: Change the statement to a present simple **question**.

1. **John puts** the cup on the shelf.   *Does John put the cup on the shelf?*
2. Mary takes the bowls to the counter. _____
3. The girls need forks. _____
4. The boys want spoons. _____
5. We wash the pots and pans. _____
6. Gina remembers the old stove. _____
7. Greg gets the refrigerator. _____
8. I get a knife. _____
9. You need a glass. _____
10. The cup goes in the cupboard. _____
11. The napkins go in the wastebasket. _____
12. The sink has dirty plates. _____
13. You need a new oven. _____
14. Tina wants your microwave. _____
15. Anne likes our kitchen. _____

basicesl.com/workbook-1/lesson-08

Exercises

C: Answer the question with *yes* answer and a short *no* answer. Use **subject pronouns** and <u>contractions</u>. Follow the example.

1. Do you have napkins? *Yes, **I** have napkins.*
   *No, **I** don't.*

2. Does the table need a tablecloth?

3. Does Fred like the plates?

4. Do the students use the oven?

5. Do I get a pencil?

6. Does Katy go to school?

7. Does the cupboard have a shelf?

8. Do the windows have blinds?

9. Does the stove get dirty?

10. Do you want another knife?

11. Does he go to school?

Workbook 1 • Lesson 8: Kitchen

Exercises

D: Read the story. Answer each question with a complete sentence.

Paula has a beautiful kitchen. Her kitchen has a big refrigerator and a new stove. It also has an oven. The counter has a microwave. Two pans and one pot are on the stove. The cupboards are for clean plates and bowls. The clean cups go on the shelf.

The dirty plates are in the sink. Paula doesn't wash the plates. Her sons do wash the plates. They put the clean plates and bowls in the cupboard. Paula puts the cups on the shelf.

The table needs a tablecloth. Paula grabs a tablecloth from the counter. She puts the tablecloth on the table. Paula gets four clean napkins for the table. She puts a fork, knife and spoon on the napkins. Paula and her sons sit at the table.

1. Does the kitchen have an oven?

   Yes, the kitchen has an oven.

2. Where do the clean cups go?

3. Where are the dirty plates?

4. Do her sons wash the plates?

5. What does the table need?

6. What does Paula put on the napkins?

basicesl.com/workbook-1/lesson-08

Exercises

E: Use the clues to form sentences. Follow the example.

1. father / <u>to need</u> / **glass**

Does father <u>need</u> a cup?

No, he <u>doesn't need</u> a cup.

What does he <u>need</u>?

*He <u>needs</u> a **glass**.*

2. Jan / to get / fork

3. Al and Pam / to want / oven

4. kitchen / to have / stove

5. I / to take / plate

Workbook 1 • Lesson 8: Kitchen

71

Exercises

F: Complete the question with *who*, *what*, *when*, *where*, or *how*.

1. Q: *Who do you get a clean plate from?* A: You get a clean plate from **John**.
   Q: *Who gets a clean plate?* A: **Kelly** gets a clean plate.

2. Q: _____ A: **Kevin** goes to the library.
   Q: _____ A: Kevin goes to the library with **Adam**.

3. Q: _____ A: **The pencil** has an eraser.
   Q: _____ A: The students have **pens**.

4. Q: _____ A: We learn **math and English** in class.
   Q: _____ A: **We** learn math and English.

5. Q: _____ A: **The mother and father** sit at the table.
   Q: _____ A: They sit at the table with **the children**.

G: Listen to the story and choose the correct answer.
Visit **basicesl.com/workbook-1/lesson-08** to listen to the story.

1. Jane and her mother have a new __*apartment*__ . a. table **(b.) apartment** c. house
2. Jane's kitchen is **not** _____ . a. dirty b. beautiful c. clean
3. The kitchen **does not have** a _____ . a. microwave b. oven c. stove
4. Jane's mother uses the _____ every day. a. pans b. spoons c. oven
5. Jane _____ the plates to the cupboard. a. moves b. uses c. takes
6. Jane's mother wants a new _____ . a. stove b. table c. tablecloth
7. The door to the patio does not _____ . a. close b. open c. small
8. Jane _____ their new apartment. a. loves b. plays c. likes

Lesson 9

Bedroom & Bathroom
Plural noun spelling rules
Possessive form of nouns

 basicesl.com/workbook-1/lesson-09

- [ ] Watch vocabulary video. Listen and repeat.
- [ ] Complete vocabulary exercises. (**Download**)
- [ ] Watch grammar video. Listen and repeat.
- [ ] Complete grammar exercises. (**Workbook**)
- [ ] Complete extra grammar exercises. (**Download**)
- [ ] Take a quiz. (**Download**)

Vocabulary

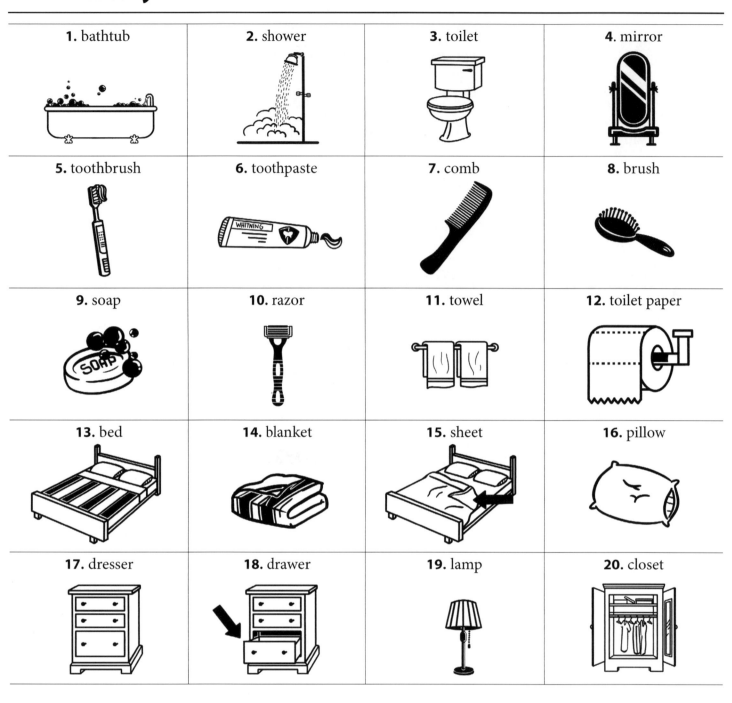

1. bathtub	2. shower	3. toilet	4. mirror
5. toothbrush	6. toothpaste	7. comb	8. brush
9. soap	10. razor	11. towel	12. toilet paper
13. bed	14. blanket	15. sheet	16. pillow
17. dresser	18. drawer	19. lamp	20. closet

21. hard (*adj*)
22. soft (*adj*)
23. neat (*adj*)
24. messy (*adj*)
25. to shower (*verb*)
26. to fold (*verb*)
27. to clean (*verb*)
28. to sleep (*verb**)
29. to look (*verb*)

* Irregular verb list page 6

Grammar

Plural noun spelling rules

For nouns ending in -ch, -sh, -s, -x, -z (and sometimes -o), add **-es**

brush → brush**es**	couch → couch**es**
glass → glass**es**	potato → potato**es**
I have one brush.	She has two **brushes**.
I need one glass.	They need two **glasses**.

For nouns ending in a *consonant* + *-y*, change the *-y* to **-ies**.

family → famil**ies**	party → part**ies**
library → librar**ies**	balcony → balcon**ies**
My school has one library.	Your school has two **libraries**.
His house has one balcony.	Her house has two **balconies**.

For nouns ending in *-f* or *-fe*, change the *-f* or *-fe* to **-ves**.

knife → kni**ves**	wife → wi**ves**
shelf → shel**ves**	life → li**ves**
Tom gets one knife.	You and Kim get two **knives**.
The cupboard has one shelf.	The closet has four **shelves**.

There are irregular plural nouns that do not follow spelling rules. Some plural nouns use the same word. Other plural nouns use different words.

man → men	woman → women
child → children	person → people
scissors → scissors	fish → fish
A child is on the bed.	The **children** are on the bed.
He is a nice person.	They are nice **people**.

Regular plural nouns end in *-s* or *-es*. There are other spelling rules that depend on the ending of the noun.

> most nouns → **-s**
> ends in *-ch, -sh, -s, -x, -z* → **-es**
> ends in consonant + *-y* → **-ies**
> ends in *-f, -fe* → **-ves**

An irregular noun is a noun that does not become plural by adding an *-s* or *-es*.

Possessive form of nouns

For most nouns we form the possessive by adding **-'s**.

John has a razor.	Mary has a house.
The razor is clean.	The house is beautiful.
John's razor is clean.	**Mary's** house is beautiful.
The girl has a pillow.	The child has a closet.
The pillow is soft.	The closet is messy.
The **girl's** pillow is soft.	The **child's** closet is messy.

For most plural nouns ending in *-s* we add an apostrophe (**-s'**).

The students have pens.	The boys have blankets.
The pens are blue.	The blankets are clean.
The **students'** pens are blue.	The **boys'** blankets are clean.
The cousins have dressers.	The teachers have desks.
The dressers are nice.	The desks are neat.
The **cousins'** dressers are nice.	The **teachers'** desks are neat.

The possessive form of nouns shows a possessive relationship between people or things. To create the possessive form, add an *apostrophe* and *-s* to the noun (**-'s**).

> the comb of the sister
> → the **sister's** comb

If the noun is plural and not irregular, or ends in *-s*, add an *apostrophe* after the noun (**-s'**).

> the beds of the sisters
> → the **sisters'** beds

Workbook 1 • Lesson 9: Bedroom & Bathroom

Exercises

A: Write the plural form of the noun.

1. glass _glasses_
2. plate _____
3. knife _____
4. balcony _____
5. toothbrush _____
6. stove _____
7. coach _____
8. microwave _____
9. library _____
10. boy _____

11. wife _____
12. party _____
13. birthday _____
14. shelf _____
15. history _____
16. glass _____
17. fork _____
18. family _____
19. table _____
20. couch _____

B: Write two sentences expressing **possession** using the given words. Follow the example.

1. Dave / towel / dirty

    The **towel of Dave** is dirty.

    **Dave's towel** is dirty.

2. Donna / pillow / soft

    _____

    _____

3. your sister / closets / big

    _____

    _____

4. the boys / bedrooms / upstairs

    _____

    _____

5. the girl / dresser / in her bedroom

    _____

    _____

basicesl.com/workbook-1/lesson-09

Exercises

C: Make the **bold** nouns **plural.** Rewrite the sentence with the correct <u>verb</u> form.

1. The **boy** <u>needs</u> a **comb**.   *The **boys** <u>need</u> **combs**.*

2. The **tray** goes on the **shelf**.   *The **trays** <u>go</u> on the **shelves**.*

3. **He** cleans **his bedroom**.

4. Is the **toilet** dirty?

5. Does the **man** clean the **shower**?

6. Is Pam's **brush** in a **drawer**?

7. Sam's **toothbrush** is on a sink.

8. **I** take the **plate** to the counter.

9. My **son** is at the library.

10. The **library** has a **book**.

11. The **boy** sleeps with the **blanket**.

12. **She** needs the **glass**.

13. **He** looks for a **razor**.

14. Alex's **house** has a **television**.

15. Does the **couch** look soft?

16. His **office** is at Frank's school.

17. **My** balcony **door** is closed.

18. The **coach** helps the **teacher**.

19. The **man** and **woman** are here.

20. The **child's gift** is at the party.

21. Do **I** put the **knife** in the drawer?

22. My **son** wants a new **towel**.

Workbook 1 • Lesson 9: Bedroom & Bathroom

Exercises

D: Form the questions for the given answers.

1. *Where is Tom?* — Tom is **in the classroom**.
2. *What does Tom learn?* — Tom learns **math**.
3. _____ — **Yes**, he **is** smart.
4. _____ — His **last name** is Jones.
5. _____ — He is **eleven years old**.
6. _____ — **No**, Tom doesn't **like** art.
7. _____ — **No**, Jane **isn't** a child.
8. _____ — Jane is **28 years old**.
9. _____ — She is **short and pretty**.
10. _____ — **Yes**, she **reads** books.
11. _____ — She reads **in her bedroom**.
12. _____ — **Yes**, her bedroom **is** downstairs.
13. _____ — **Yes**, she **likes** her bedroom.
14. _____ — John is **my brother**.
15. _____ — He is **18 years old**.
16. _____ — **Yes**, I **love** my brother.
17. _____ — **No**, John **isn't** married.
18. _____ — **Yes,** he **is** handsome.
19. _____ — John's room is **upstairs**.

basicesl.com/workbook-1/lesson-09

Exercises

E: Read the story and answer the questions. Use complete sentences. Follow the example.

Kim's home is big and beautiful. Her favorite rooms are the kitchen and the bedroom. Kim's bedroom is upstairs and the kitchen is downstairs. One bathroom is upstairs. Another bathroom is downstairs.

The kitchen has a stove, a microwave and a refrigerator. Kim uses the toaster on the counter. She doesn't have a blender. The kitchen table is nice. It has a pretty tablecloth. Kim doesn't put dirty dishes on the counter. She puts dirty dishes in the sink.

Her bedroom is neat. She has blinds on the windows. A mirror is on the dresser. Kim's bed is very soft. She sleeps well in her bed. Kim loves pillows. She has eight pillows on the bed. She wants new sheets. She has three blankets in the closet.

1. Are Kim's favorite rooms the kitchen and the bedroom?

   Yes, her favorite rooms are the kitchen and the bedroom.

2. Where is Kim's bedroom?

   _____

3. How many bathrooms does Kim's home have?

   _____

4. What does Kim use on the counter?

   _____

5. Where does Kim put the dirty dishes?

   _____

6. Is Kim's bedroom messy?

   _____

7. Does Kim have a blanket in the closet?

   _____

Workbook 1 • Lesson 9: Bedroom & Bathroom

Exercises

F: Fill in the blanks with the possessive plural form. Follow the example.

1. I have one daughter. Her bedroom is messy.

My _____*daughter's*_____ _____*bedroom*_____ is messy.

2. I have one house. Its bedrooms are upstairs.

My _____ _____ are upstairs.

3. You go to two schools. Their playgrounds are fun.

Your _____ _____ are fun.

4. I study at one library. The books are boring.

The _____ _____ are boring.

5. Alice has five children. Their cousins are polite.

The _____ _____ are polite.

6. Alice has four girls. Their uncle is funny.

The _____ _____ is funny.

G: Listen to the story and choose the correct answer.
Visit **basicesl.com/workbook-1/lesson-09** to listen to the story.

1. Jen is Pam's ___*sister*___ .   a. friend   b. mother   (c.) sister

2. Jen's bedroom has two _____ .   a. dressers   b. lamps   c. pillows

3. Jen's closet has a mirror and _____ .   a. a shelf   b. shelves   c. a drawer

4. Their bathroom is **not** _____ .   a. pretty   b. dirty   c. big

5. The glass on the sink is for _____ .   a. toothbrushes b. combs   c. razors

6. Pam's towels are in the _____ .   a. dresser   b. cupboard   c. closet

7. Jen's towels are in the _____ .   a. dresser   b. cupboard   c. closet

8. The old brushes are in the _____ .   a. drawer   b. wastebasket   c. sink

basicesl.com/workbook-1/lesson-09

Lesson 10

Clothes

Using *this*, *that*, *these* and *those*
Questions about possession with the word *whose*

 basicesl.com/workbook-1/lesson-10

- ☐ Watch vocabulary video. Listen and repeat.
- ☐ Complete vocabulary exercises. (**Download**)
- ☐ Watch grammar video. Listen and repeat.
- ☐ Complete grammar exercises. (**Workbook**)
- ☐ Complete extra grammar exercises. (**Download**)
- ☐ Take a quiz. (**Download**)

Vocabulary

1. clothes	2. shirt	3. T-shirt	4. tank top
5. pants	6. jeans	7. shorts	8. skirt
9. suit	10. dress	11. jacket	12. sweater
13. shoes	14. sandals	15. socks	16. hat
17. underwear	18. bra	19. pajamas	20. robe

21. new (*adj*)
22. used (*adj*)
23. favorite (*adj*)
24. to hate (*verb*)
25. to choose (*verb**)
26. to share (*verb*)
27. to prefer (*verb*)
28. to lose (*verb**)
29. to wear (*verb**)

* Irregular verb list page 6

Grammar

Using *this*, *that*, *these* and *those*

Singular and near
This sweater is red.
This skirt is beautiful.
He prefers **this** shirt.
I want **this** robe.

Singular and not near
That sweater is blue.
That skirt is ugly.
He doesn't prefer **that** shirt.
I don't want **that** robe.

Plural and near
These sweaters are new.
These clothes are clean.
Jenny wears **these** jeans.
You need **these** shoes.

Plural and not near
Those sweaters are used.
Those clothes are dirty.
Jenny doesn't wear **those** jeans.
You don't need **those** shoes.

Adjective
This jacket is old.
Is **this** tank top ugly?

Mary likes **that** dress.
Is **that** hat blue?

These jeans aren't new.
Are **these** socks clean?

Those clothes are messy.
Do **those** shoes look ugly?

Pronoun
This is old.
Is **this** ugly?

Mary likes **that**.
Is **that** blue?

These aren't new.
Are **these** clean?

Those are messy.
Do **those** look ugly?

Demonstrative adjectives are used to point out specific people or things.

The words *this* and *that* are used with **singular** nouns. The words *these* and *those* are used with **plural** nouns.

Singular	Plural
this hat	**these** hats
that hat	**those** hats

This and *these* are used with nouns that are **near**. *That* and *those* are used with nouns that are **not near**.

Near	Not near
this hat	**that** hat
these hats	**those** hats

This, *that*, *these* and *those* can also be used as pronouns. Pronouns are used to substitute nouns.

Questions about possession with *whose*

Whose green shirt is this?   It's **Helen's** shirt.
                                  That is **Helen's** shirt.

Whose robe is that?   It's **John's** robe.
                                  This robe is **John's**.

Whose sandals are these?   They are my **daughter's** sandals.
                                  Those are my **daughter's**.

Whose socks are those?   They are the **boys'** socks.
                                  These socks are the **boys'**.

Whose child is this?   She is **Jacob's** child.
                                  This child is **Jacob's**.

The question word *whose* is used to find out who something belongs to.

Demonstratives and the possessive form of nouns can be used to answer questions about possession.

Workbook 1 • Lesson 10: Clothes

Exercises

A: Complete the sentence with *this, that, these* or *those*.

1. (near) I love __these__ pants.
2. (not near) I don't like _____ pants.
3. (near) She prefers _____ socks.
4. (not near) _____ socks are ugly.
5. (not near) _____ shirt is red.
6. (near) She hates _____ skirt.
7. (not near) He prefers _____ sweaters.
8. (near) I don't share _____ hat.
9. (near) Do you wear _____ shorts?
10. (not near) _____ old robe is soft.
11. (near) _____ jacket is new.
12. (not near) _____ suit is my favorite.

B: Is it an **adjective** or a **pronoun**?

1. __adjective__ Do you like **this** hat?
2. __pronoun__ I like **those**.
3. _____ They share **these** clothes.
4. _____ Does he wear **this**?
5. _____ **These** shoes are old.
6. _____ Aren't **those** Mary's?
7. _____ How old is **that**?
8. _____ **That** robe is two years old.
9. _____ How old are **these**?
10. _____ **This** shirt is ugly.
11. _____ Do you prefer **that**?
12. _____ **Those** sandals are nice.

C: Use the clues to write a statement. Follow the example.

1. near / dirty — *This is a dirty hat.*
2. not near / ugly
3. near / clean
4. not near / nice
5. not near / old
6. near / soft

www.basicesl.com/workbook-1/lesson-10

84

Exercises

D: Rewrite the sentence. Use an opposite adjective.

1. *This* skirt is *beautiful*.   <u>*That* skirt is **ugly**.</u>
2. *These* shoes are *white*.   _____
3. *Those* T-shirts are *new*.   _____
4. *These* pajamas are *clean*.   _____
5. *That* closet isn't *messy*.   _____
6. *That* jacket is *small*.   _____
7. *This* bed is *hard*.   _____
8. *These* sandals aren't *good*.   _____
9. *Those* questions are *easy*.   _____
10. *That* book is *serious*.   _____

E: Write the question for the given answer. Use the <u>opposite</u> demonstrative adjective. Follow example.

1. Q: <u>***Do* you *like* that jacket?**</u>   A: **Yes**, I **like** <u>this</u> jacket.
2. Q: _____   A: *That* sweater is **blue**.
3. Q: _____   A: **Yes**, *this* **is** my favorite suit.
4. Q: _____   A: **No**, I **don't like** *that* hat.
5. Q: _____   A: *Those* are **my sister's** sweaters.
6. Q: _____   A: **Yes**, I **like** *these* shoes.
7. Q: _____   A: *This* green skirt is **Mary's skirt**.
8. Q: _____   A: **No**, *these* sandals **aren't** new.
9. Q: _____   A: *These* sandals are **two years old**
10. Q: _____   A: I keep *that* robe **in my room**.

Workbook 1 • Lesson 10: Clothes

Exercises

F: Read the story and answer the questions.

Mother: Alex and Bobby, this bedroom is messy. Whose dirty clothes are these?

Alex: Those dirty jeans on the floor are Bobby's. My jeans are clean. They are on the bed.

Mother: Whose black underwear and green towel are in the bathroom?

Bobby: Those are Alex's underwear. He has black underwear. My underwear are white.

Alex: Mom, those are Bobby's underwear and towel. He wears my black underwear. His white underwear are dirty. He uses the green towels. I use the red towels.

Mother: Bobby take these dirty clothes downstairs to the garage.

1. Whose room is messy?

   Alex and Bobby's room is messy.

2. Whose dirty jeans are those on the floor?

   _____

3. Where are the clean jeans?

   _____

4. Whose underwear is black?

   _____

5. Who uses green towels?

   _____

6. Where does Bobby take the dirty clothes?

   _____

www.basicesl.com/workbook-1/lesson-10

Exercises

G: Follow the example. Use the given clues.

1. the boys / to wear / **near**

Do the boys wear **these** clothes?

No, they don't wear **these** clothes.

What clothes do the boys wear?

They wear <u>those</u> clothes.

2. Cynthia / to hate / **near**

3. you / to prefer / **not near**

4. Robert / to choose / **near**

5. I / to take / **not near**

Workbook 1 • Lesson 10: Clothes

Exercises

H: Listen to the story and choose the correct answer.
Visit **www.basicesl.com/workbook-1/lesson-10** to listen to the story.

1. Tanya loves her new ___clothes___ .

                a. pants   **(b.)** clothes   **c.** skirts

2. She _____ old jeans and sweaters.

                a. wears   **b.** shares   **c.** loses

3. Tanya doesn't share her _____ clothes.

                a. favorite   **b.** old   **c.** new

4. Gina _____ Tanya's old clothes.

                a. loses   **b.** wears   **c.** hates

5. Gina loves Tanya's _____ .

                a. bedroom   **b.** closet   **c.** jeans

6. Tanya has a new _____ .

                a. tank top   **b.** hat   **c.** skirt

7. Tanya's favorite skirt is _____ .

                a. red   **b.** orange   **c.** yellow

8. Tanya's skirt goes with Gina's _____ .

                a. sandals   **b.** sweater   **c.** tank top

www.basicesl.com/workbook-1/lesson-10

Lesson 11

Style
Word substitution with *one* and *ones*
Questions about choice with *which*
Asking about order

 basicesl.com/workbook-1/lesson-11

- [ ] Watch vocabulary video. Listen and repeat.
- [ ] Complete vocabulary exercises. (**Download**)
- [ ] Watch grammar video. Listen and repeat.
- [ ] Complete grammar exercises. (**Workbook**)
- [ ] Complete extra grammar exercises. (**Download**)
- [ ] Take a quiz. (**Download**)

Vocabulary

1. button	2. zipper	3. pocket	4. collar
5. belt	6. scarf	7. gloves	8. purse
9. wallet	10. watch	11. earring	12. necklace
13. tight (adj)	14. loose (adj)	15. comfortable (adj)	16. uncomfortable (adj)
17. casual (adj)	18. formal (adj)	19. solid (adj)	20. striped (adj)

21. size (noun)
22. small (adj)
23. medium (adj)
24. large (adj)
25. extra (adj)
26. to keep (verb*)
27. to pick (verb)
28. to find (verb*)
29. to come (verb*)

Irregular verb list page 6

basicesl.com/workbook-1/lesson-11

Grammar

Word substitution with *one* and *ones*

I have a new *wallet*.	You have an old **one**.
We buy used *watches*.	They buy new **ones**.
Donald wears a striped *suit*.	Roger wears a solid **one**.
Ellen prefers large *buttons*.	Erin prefers small **ones**.
You want a formal *jacket*.	I want a casual **one**.
The boys have blue *gloves*.	The girls have pink **ones**.

Question	Answer
Is this *shirt* loose?	Yes, that **one** is loose.
Does Kim need a *sweater*?	No, she doesn't need **one**.
Do you have a *necklace*?	Yes, I have a silver **one**.
Does Bob find a new *watch*?	No, he doesn't find a new **one**.
Are the big *earrings* pretty?	Yes, the big **ones** are pretty.
Do they come to this *store*?	No, they don't come to this **one**.

The words *one* and *ones* are often used as pronouns. Pronouns are used to substitute nouns. The pronouns *one* and *ones* are used to avoid repetition.

hat → **one**
hats → **ones**

Questions about choice with *which*

Question	Answer
Which scarf does Judy prefer?	She prefers **the extra large scarf**.
Which collar is uncomfortable?	**The tight one** is uncomfortable.
Which shirt does Henry like?	He likes **the casual shirt**.
Which jackets do they keep?	They keep **the clean ones**.
Which gloves are torn?	**The gloves on the bed** are torn.
Which belt comes with the dress?	**The red one** comes with the dress.

The question word *which* is used to ask about choice or preference. The answer is a specific person or thing from a group.

Asking about order

Which hat does Greg pick?
He picks the **first** one.

Which dress is a size medium?
The **second** one is medium.

Which of these pants are clean?
The **third** ones are clean.

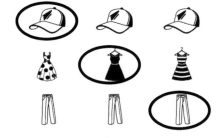

Question	Answer
Where do the new purses go?	They go on the **fourth** rack.
When is the sale?	It is on the **fifth** day of October.
Which customer is Tom?	He is the **sixth** customer in line.

Ordinal numbers are used to show order or position.

one (1) → **first** (1st)
two (2) → **second** (2nd)
three (3) → **third** (3rd)
four (4) → **fourth** (4th)
five (5) → **fifth** (5th)
six (6) → **sixth** (6th)

7th - seventh	**13th** - thirteenth	**19th** - nineteenth
8th - eighth	**14th** - fourteenth	**20th** - twentieth
9th - ninth	**15th** - fifteenth	**21st** - twenty-first
10th - tenth	**16th** - sixteenth	**22nd** - twenty-second
11th - eleventh	**17th** - seventeenth	**23rd** - twenty-third
12th - twelfth	**18th** - eighteenth	**24th** - twenty-fourth

Workbook 1 • Lesson 11: Style

Exercises

A: Complete the sentence with *one* or *ones*.

1. I like red *buttons*. Mary likes blue __*ones*__ . a. one (b.) ones
2. We have fancy *earrings*. Mom has casual _____ . a. one b. ones
3. My shirt has a red *collar*. Stan's shirt has a blue _____ . a. one b. ones
4. Alan wants a new *wallet*. Do you want _____ ? a. one b. ones
5. Emma prefers tight *jeans*. I prefer loose _____ . a. one b. ones
6. They have an old *blanket*. You have a new _____ . a. one b. ones
7. I prefer large *pockets*. You prefer small _____ . a. one b. ones
8. Dan has a gold *watch*. Nancy has a silver _____ . a. one b. ones
9. This *shirt* is torn. That _____ is not torn. a. one b. ones
10. The red *gloves* are cheap. These _____ are not cheap. a. one b. ones

B: Write the ordinal number.

1. **1st** __*first*__
2. **2nd** _____
3. **3rd** _____
4. **4th** _____
5. **5th** _____
6. **6th** _____
7. **7th** _____
8. **8th** _____
9. **9th** _____
10. **10th** _____
11. **11th** _____
12. **12th** _____
13. **33rd** _____
14. **41st** _____
15. **99th** _____
16. **72nd** _____
17. **86th** _____
18. **13th** _____
19. **22nd** _____
20. **18th** _____

basicesl.com/workbook-1/lesson-11

Exercises

C: Form a question using **which** and an answer with a <u>one</u> or <u>ones</u> substitution for the noun.

1. scarf / Ann / want —— *Which scarf does Ann want?*

   fancy —— *She wants the **fancy one**.*

2. suits / Jim and Mike / share ——

   striped ——

3. jacket / you / like ——

   red ——

4. buttons / I / get ——

   large ——

5. earrings / Sara / need ——

   small ——

D: Write a **negative** sentence using an <u>opposite</u> adjective and <u>one</u> or <u>ones</u> substitution. Follow the example.

1. **Shelly wears** <u>black socks</u>. —— *She doesn't wear <u>white ones</u>.*
2. **Jane and I like** your <u>new sweater</u>. —— *We don't like your <u>old one</u>.*
3. **I use** my <u>old coat</u>. ——
4. **Al and Ted need** <u>easy questions</u>. ——
5. **The plate goes** in the <u>big sink</u>. ——
6. **Amy keeps** her <u>pretty skirts</u>. ——
7. **My son has** <u>loose jeans</u>. ——
8. **You erase** the <u>wrong answers</u>. ——
9. **You and Tim have** the <u>funny book</u>. ——
10. **I sleep** in a <u>little bed</u>. ——

Exercises

E: Rewrite the story. Change *sister* to **sisters**. Use noun substitution for words in bold.

My sister has two closets. She has a large closet and a small **closet**. She keeps her favorite dresses in the large closet. She keeps her favorite sweaters in the small **closet**.

My sister's favorite dresses are the solid **dresses**. She wears the solid dresses to school. She does not wear the fancy **dresses** to school.

My sister also loves sandals. She has brown sandals, black sandals, and white **sandals**. The black and white sandals are tight. The brown **sandals** are comfortable.

My sister has jeans she doesn't wear. She doesn't wear the extra small jeans. She also doesn't wear the torn **jeans**.

*My **sisters**...*

Exercises

F: Follow the example. Use the given clues.

1. Fred / to like

    Which belt does Fred like?

    Fred likes the **third** belt.

    He doesn't like the **first** <u>one</u>.

2. I / to need

3. Lisa / to want

4. Jim & I / to take

5. Kelly / to wear

6. I / to love / You

Workbook 1 • Lesson 11: Style

Exercises

G: Listen to the story and choose the correct answer.
Visit **basicesl.com/workbook-1/lesson-11** to listen to the story.

1. Ellen has ___three___ new shirts.

    a. one   **b.** two   **c.** three ⃝

2. The _____ shirt is a formal shirt.

    a. first   **b.** second   **c.** third

3. The formal shirt is a _____ white shirt.

    a. solid   **b.** striped   **c.** ugly

4. The formal shirt has six black _____ .

    a. zippers   **b.** buttons   **c.** belts

5. The casual shirt is _____ .

    a. tight   **b.** comfortable   **c.** loose

6. The casual shirt is size _____ .

    a. large   **b.** medium   **c.** small

7. The T-shirt is size _____ .

    a. large   **b.** medium   **c.** small

8. The T-shirt is solid red and _____ .

    a. tight   **b.** loose   **c.** extra

basicesl.com/workbook-1/lesson-11

Lesson 12

Shopping
Prepositions of time and place
Prepositions and prepositional phrases

 basicesl.com/workbook-1/lesson-12

- ☐ Watch vocabulary video. Listen and repeat.
- ☐ Complete vocabulary exercises. (**Download**)
- ☐ Watch grammar video. Listen and repeat.
- ☐ Complete grammar exercises. (**Workbook**)
- ☐ Complete extra grammar exercises. (**Download**)
- ☐ Take a quiz. (**Download**)

Vocabulary

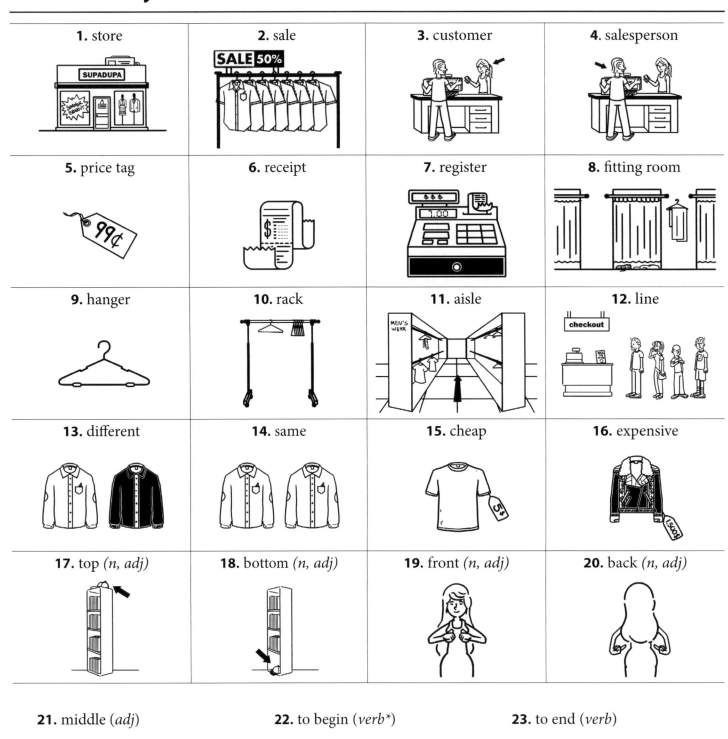

21. middle (*adj*)
22. to begin (*verb**)
23. to end (*verb*)
24. to sell (*verb**)
25. to buy (*verb**)
26. to pay (*verb**)
27. to return (*verb*)
28. to help (*verb*)
29. to shop (*verb*)

Irregular verb list page 6

Grammar

Prepositions of time and place

Time: *in, on* and *at*

When does the store open?
 The store opens **in** March.
 The store opens **in** a few years.
 It opens **in** the morning.

When are the lines short?
 The lines are short **on** Fridays.
 They are short **on** weekends.
 They are short **on** July 4th.

When does the sale begin?
 The sale begins **at** midnight.
 The sale begins **at** 10:00 a.m.
 It begins **at** noon.

Place: *in, on* and *at*

Where is the customer?
 The customer is **in** the store.
 The customer is **in** line.
 She is **in** the fitting room.

Where are the cheap shirts?
 The cheap shirts are **on** aisle ten.
 Those are **on** the second floor.
 They are **on** these shelves.

Where is the salesperson?
 She is **at the back** of the store.
 He is **at the front** of the store.
 She is **at the register**.

Where are the sale racks?
 The sale racks are **by** the door.
 They are **along** the wall.

Where is the price tag?
 The price tag is **inside** the shirt.
 It is **beside** the collar.

When does the store close?
 It closes **from** 2:00 **to** 4:00.
 The store closes **after** midnight.

Where are my hangers?
 They are **on top of** the bed.
 They are **under** the bed.

Where are the expensive dresses?
 They are **near** the door.
 Those are **across** the store.

When is the salesperson back?
 He is back **between** 6 and 9.
 She is back **around** 1:30 p.m.

Prepositions show relationships between people, places, and things. For example, prepositions help describe time or place.

There are many common prepositions like *in*, *at* and *on* that are used in every day language.

Time
in → months and years
on → days and dates
at → specific times

Place
in → enclosed spaces
on → surfaces
at → specific points

Prepositions are usually placed in front of nouns or pronouns. This is known as a prepositional phrase.

 ... **in** the store.

There are other prepositions that are used to express more specific information about time or place.

Prepositions and prepositional phrases

above	**above** the counter	before	**before** Wednesday
below	**below** the counter	after	**after** Wednesday
up	**up** the stairs	with	**with** socks
down	**down** the stairs	without	**without** socks
inside	**inside** the pocket	on	**on** the hanger
outside	**outside** the pocket	off	**off** the hanger
in front of	**in front of** the register	over	**over** the fence
behind	**behind** the register	under	**under** the fence
along	**along** the aisle	between	**between** the racks
across	**across** the aisle	beside	**beside** the rack
near (by)	**near (by)** the store	around	**around** the line
far from	**far from** the store	through	**through** the line

Prepositions are used to describe place, direction, time and more.

Some prepositions are related or have opposite meanings.

Workbook 1 • Lesson 12: Shopping

Exercises

A: Complete the sentence using *in*, *at* or *on*.

1. The store opens __at__ noon.
2. It goes _____ the table.
3. The new store opens _____ 2020.
4. He is _____ the bedroom.
5. The store opens _____ 10:00 a.m.
6. He returns his hat _____ the store.
7. The sandals are _____ sale.
8. The salesperson is _____ the register.
9. The customers are _____ line.
10. The shirts are _____ the hangers.
11. Tia is _____ the fitting room.
12. The gloves are _____ the shelf.

B: Write an opposite word or phrase.

1. top __bottom__
2. over _____
3. behind _____
4. with _____
5. down _____
6. below _____
7. off _____
8. before _____
9. cheap _____
10. outside _____
11. different _____
12. in the front of _____

C: Complete the story using prepositions.

Tom needs new shoes __for__ school. His shoes are old and dirty. Tom's shoes get dirty
(for / to)

_____ school _____ the playground. Tom keeps his old shoes _____ the garage.
(on / at)   (on / at)   (around / inside)

Tom puts his shoes _____ a table _____ the door.
(below / bottom)   (in / by)

Tom buys shoes _____ the shoe store. Tom's favorite shoe store is _____ his
(at / on)   (around / near)

school. The store sells shoes _____ men and women. The men's shoes are _____
(for / in)   (at the back of / with)

the store. The store also sells socks and sandals. The socks are _____ a shelf _____
(on / in)   (behind / in)

the register. The sandals are _____ the store.
(at the front of / over)

basicesl.com/workbook-1/lesson-12

Exercises

D: Use the image to answer the questions. Follow the example.

1. The customer is __in/inside__ the store.
   - a. in
   - b. inside
   - c. on
   - d. a & b ✓

2. The shoes are _____ the shelves.
   - a. in
   - b. under
   - c. on
   - d. far from

3. The fitting room is _____ the shelves.
   - a. after
   - b. before
   - c. behind
   - d. along

4. The woman is _____ the rack with white pants.
   - a. in front of
   - b. behind
   - c. to
   - d. without

5. A child is _____ the shelf.
   - a. between
   - b. under
   - c. on top of
   - d. around

6. The coats are _____ the wall.
   - a. under
   - b. along
   - c. between
   - d. through

7. The salesperson is _____ the rack.
   - a. behind
   - b. below
   - c. beside
   - d. with

8. The purses are _____ the coats.
   - a. under
   - b. around
   - c. below
   - d. a & c

Workbook 1 • Lesson 12: Shopping

Exercises

E: Use a **preposition** to describe the picture. Follow the example.

1.    *The price tag is **on** the shirt.*

   price tag / shirt

2.    _____

   salesperson / register

3.    _____

   customer / store

4. 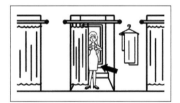   _____

   woman / fitting room

5.    _____

   scarves / purses

6. 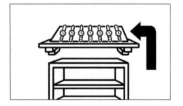   _____

   watches / shelf

basicesl.com/workbook-1/lesson-12

Exercises

F: Use the image to answer the questions. Follow the example.

1. Where is the register? (counter)

   *The register is **on** the counter.*

2. Where is the couch? (room)

3. Where is the woman? (mirror)

4. Where is the salesperson? (register)

5. Where are the shelves? (store) (wall)

6. Where is the wastebasket? (floor) (counter)

Workbook 1 • Lesson 12: Shopping

Exercises

G: Listen to the story and choose the correct answer.
Visit **basicesl.com/workbook-1/lesson-12** to listen to the story.

1. Ruby likes _formal_ dresses.

            a. formal **b.** cheap **c.** fancy

2. A dress store _____ her house is Ruby's favorite.

            a. behind **b.** far from **c.** near

3. Ruby's favorite dress store sells _____ dresses.

            a. cheap **b.** expensive **c.** ugly

4. Stores with cheap dresses are _____ her house.

            a. along **b.** far from **c.** near.

5. Ruby shops at her favorite store with her _____ .

            a. mother **b.** aunt **c.** sister

6. The formal dresses are _____ of the store.

            a. at the front **b.** at the back **c.** on the top

7. Ruby prefers a blue dress. The dress is _____ .

            a. on sale **b.** in sale **c.** off sale

8. Ruby's mother _____ for the dress at the register.

            a. buys **b.** shops **c.** pays

basicesl.com/workbook-1/lesson-12

Lesson 13

City
Present continuous statements
Present participle spelling rules (*-ing* form)

 basicesl.com/workbook-1/lesson-13

- ☐ Watch vocabulary video. Listen and repeat.
- ☐ Complete vocabulary exercises. (**Download**)
- ☐ Watch grammar video. Listen and repeat.
- ☐ Complete grammar exercises. (**Workbook**)
- ☐ Complete extra grammar exercises. (**Download**)
- ☐ Take a quiz. (**Download**)

Vocabulary

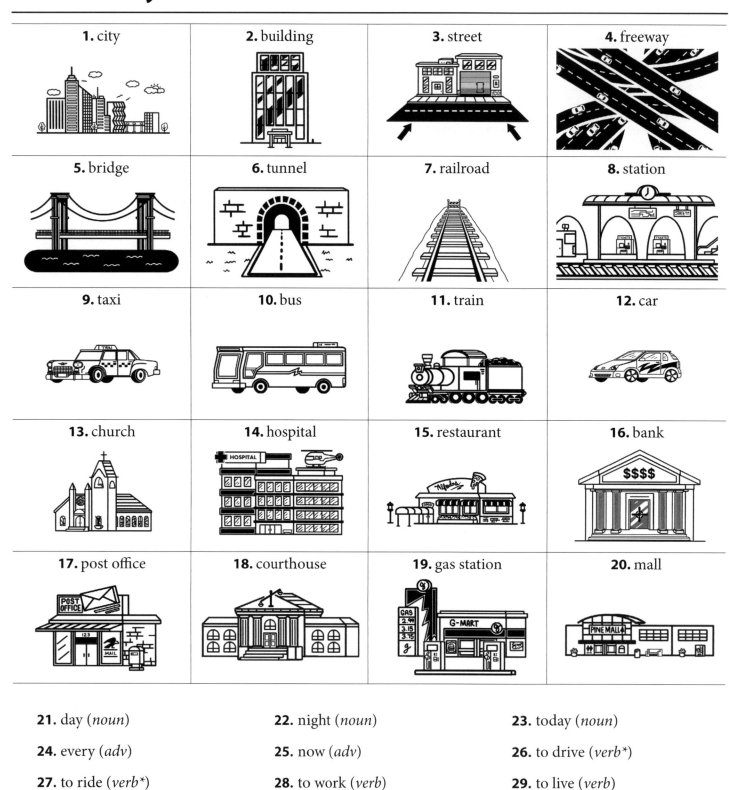

21. day (*noun*)
22. night (*noun*)
23. today (*noun*)
24. every (*adv*)
25. now (*adv*)
26. to drive (*verb**)
27. to ride (*verb**)
28. to work (*verb*)
29. to live (*verb*)

* Irregular verb list page 6

Grammar

Present continuous statements

Present Simple	Present Continuous
I listen	I *am* **listening**
You shop	You *are* **shopping**
He laughs	He *is* **laughing**
She sleeps	She *is* **sleeping**
It opens	It *is* **opening**
We learn	We *are* **learning**
They clean	They *are* **cleaning**

Present Simple	Present Continuous
I walk to church every day.	I *am* **walking** to church now.
You ride the train every day.	You *are* **riding** the bus today.
He comes to the bank on Tuesday.	He *is* **coming** to the bank now.
She helps at the hospital.	She *is* **helping** at the hospital today.
It goes down the railroad.	It *is* **going** down the railroad now.
We drive through tunnels.	We *are* **driving** through a tunnel now.
They close the restaurant at 9.	They *are* **closing** the restaurant now.

The present continuous tense is used to express an ongoing action happening now.

A present continuous statement is formed with the verb *to be* and the present participle of the main verb.

to be + **present participle**

The present participle is also known as the *-ing* **form.**

walk → **walking**

Present participle spelling rules (*-ing* form)

For most verbs, the present participle is formed by adding *-ing* to the base form of the verb.

go → go**ing**	work → work**ing**
walk → walk**ing**	return → return**ing**
I am **going** to church on Sunday.	He is **working** at the court house.
You are **walking** on the street.	We are **returning** to the post office.

For verbs ending in a silent *e*, drop the *-e* before adding *-ing*.

ride → rid**ing**	close → clos**ing**
drive → driv**ing**	take → tak**ing**
Sara is **riding** in my car.	The city is **closing** the tunnel.
Jose is **driving** on the freeway.	I am **taking** a taxi at the station.

For verbs ending in *-ie*, change the *-ie* to a *-y* before adding *-ing*.

tie → t**ying**	die → d**ying**
lie → l**ying**	
The boy is **tying** his shoes.	People are **dying** at the hospital.

For one syllable verbs that end in a vowel followed by a consonant other than *-y*, double the consonant and add *-ing*.

put → put**ting**	shop → shop**ping**
sit → sit**ting**	get → get**ting**
I am **putting** my shirt on.	The girls are **shopping** at the mall.
We are **sitting** at the cafe.	They are **getting** off the bus.

The present participle (*-ing* form) is formed by adding *-ing* to the base form of the main verb.

There are some spelling rules that depend on the ending of the verb.

walk → walk**ing**
   add *-ing*

ride → rid**ing**
   drop *-e,* add *-ing*

lie → **lying**
   change *-ie* to *-y,* add *-ing*

shop → shop**ping**
   double consonant, add *-ing*

Workbook 1 • Lesson 13: City

Exercises

A: Write the **present participle (-ing form)** of the given verb.

1. walk _walking_
2. come _____
3. learn _____
4. love _____
5. read _____
6. get _____
7. forget _____
8. do _____
9. work _____
10. drive _____
11. sit _____
12. sell _____
13. buy _____
14. need _____
15. play _____
16. pick _____
17. put _____
18. share _____
19. write _____
20. wear _____
21. prefer _____
22. begin _____

B: Write the **present continuous** form. Use the given verb and subject pronoun.

1. grab I _am grabbing_
2. study You _____
3. wear He _____
4. live She _____
5. stand It _____
6. add We _____
7. laugh They _____
8. get I _____
9. listen You _____
10. choose He _____
11. put She _____
12. help It _____
13. sleep We _____
14. answer They _____
15. talk I _____
16. write You _____
17. look He _____
18. shop She _____
19. clean It _____
20. form We _____
21. close They _____
22. open I _____

basicesl.com/workbook-1/lesson-13

Exercises

C: Write the statement in the **present continuous**. Use the word **now**. Follow the example

1. I walk to school. *I **am walking** to school **now**.*
2. You drive to church. _____
3. He rides a train. _____
4. She works in a hospital. _____
5. We live near the train station. _____
6. They shop at the dress store. _____
7. The taxi goes over the bridge. _____
8. Ray walks along the railroad. _____

D: Write a **simple present** and **present continuous** statement. Use the given clues. Follow the example.

1. *Tom **works** at the restaurant **on weekends**.*
   (Tom / to work / on weekends)
   *He **is working** at the restaurant **today**.*
   (today)

2. _____
   (Mary / to walk / on Mondays)
   _____
   (this morning)

3. _____
   (I / to go / to 10:00 a.m.)
   _____
   (now)

4. _____
   (Sarah and Jan / help / on Fridays)
   _____
   (today)

Workbook 1 • Lesson 13: City

Exercises

E: Rewrite the story. Change the simple present tense to the **present continuous** tense. Change *every day* to *today*.

I go to the mall every day with my mother and sister. We take the train to the mall. We ride the train through a tunnel and over a bridge. I sit next to the window every day. My sister stands by the door. My mother reads her book on the train every day.

*I **am going** to the mall **today**...*

My mother goes to church with her friend *every day*. They help at the church. My mother teaches English to children from different countries. My mother's friend takes people to the hospital from the church every day. They ride in a bus across the city.

*My mother **is going** ...*

basicesl.com/workbook-1/lesson-13

Exercises

F: Follow the example.

1. your aunt / to work

*Where does your aunt **work**?*

*My aunt **works** at the courthouse.*

***She's working** at the courthouse **now**.*

2. Henry / to go

3. you / to walk

4. Ann and Al / to study

5. Sylvia / to drive

6. the train / to go

Workbook 1 • Lesson 13: City

Exercises

G: Listen to the story and choose the correct answer.
Visit **basicesl.com/workbook-1/lesson-13** to listen to the story.

1. Henry and his wife ride the ___train___ into the city.

    a. taxi   **b.** bus   **(c.)** train

2. They work at the _____ every day.

    a. bank   **b.** courthouse   **c.** mall

3. Today the train did not _____ .

    a. come   **b.** drive   **c.** ride

4. Today Henry and his wife are taking a _____ .

    a. taxi   **b.** bus   **c.** car

5. Henry's children ride the _____ to school.

    a. taxi   **b.** bus   **c.** train

6. The children's school is _____ their house.

    a. far from   **b.** close to   **c.** next to

7. The bus is driving over a _____ today.

    a. railroad   **b.** street   **c.** bridge

8. Alex is _____ for a test on the bus.

    a. learning   **b.** studying   **c.** reading

Lesson 14

Traveling
Present continuous negative statements
Present continuous questions

 basicesl.com/workbook-1/lesson-14

- [ ] Watch vocabulary video. Listen and repeat.
- [ ] Complete vocabulary exercises. (**Download**)
- [ ] Watch grammar video. Listen and repeat.
- [ ] Complete grammar exercises. (**Workbook**)
- [ ] Complete extra grammar exercises. (**Download**)
- [ ] Take a quiz. (**Download**)

Workbook 1 • Lesson 14: Traveling

Vocabulary

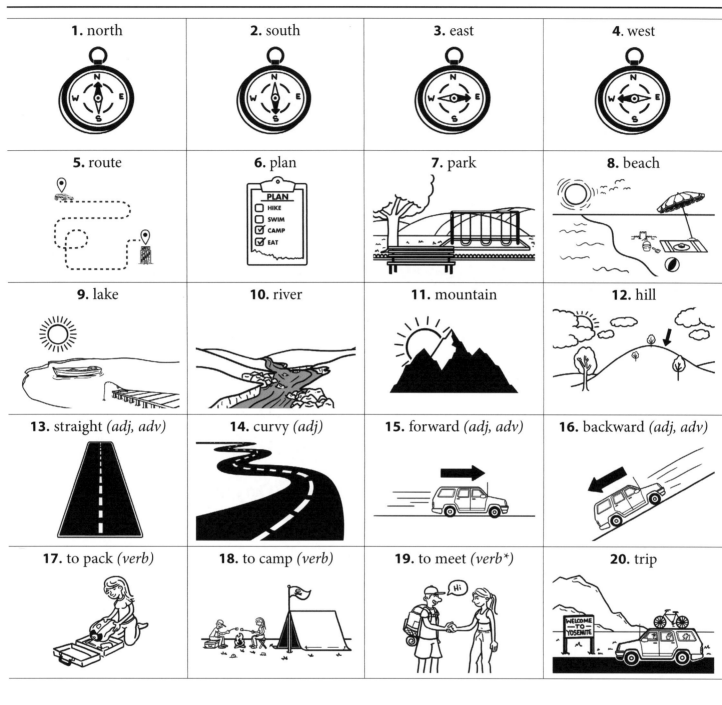

21. tonight (*noun*)
22. tomorrow (*noun*)
23. to start (*noun*)
24. to finish (*verb*)
25. to stay (*verb*)
26. to leave (*verb**)
27. to plan (*verb*)
28. to visit (*verb*)
29. to travel (*verb*)

Irregular verb list page 6

Grammar

Present continuous negative statements

Present continuous	Negative present continuous
I **am planning** a trip.	I **am** not **planning** a trip.
You **are driving** north.	You **are** not **driving** north.
He **is traveling** to Japan.	He **is** not **traveling** to Japan.
She **is visiting** her parents.	She **is** not **visiting** her parents.
It **is moving** backward.	It **is** not **moving** backward.
We **are meeting** by the river.	We **are** not **meeting** by the river.
They **are packing** for the beach.	They **are** not **packing** for the beach.

Simple present	Negative present continuous
I visit my aunt every weekend.	I **am** not **visiting** my aunt today.
He uses the shower at night.	He **is** not **using** the shower now.
She camps outside at night.	She **isn't camping** outside tonight.
We help the boys every day.	We **are** not **helping** the boys now.
They shop on Saturdays.	They **aren't shopping** tomorrow.

Negative present continuous statements express ongoing actions not happening now.

Present continuous statements use the verb *to be* and the present participle (*-ing* form) of the main verb. The word *not* is used to make the statement negative.

subject + **to be** (*not*) + **-*ing* form**

Present continuous questions

Statement	Question
I **am moving** forward.	**Am** I **moving** forward?
You **are riding** the bus home.	**Are** you **riding** the bus home?
He **is meeting** his friends.	**Is** he **meeting** his friends?
She **is driving** to Mexico.	**Is** she **driving** to Mexico?
It **is going** east along the river.	**Is** it **going** east along the river?
We **are leaving** now.	**Are** we **leaving** now?
They **are visiting** two parks.	**Are** they **visiting** two parks?

Question	Answer
Are you **leaving**?	Yes, I am.
When are you leaving?	I am leaving **now**.
Are you **visiting** Tom?	No, I'm not.
Who are you visiting?	I am visiting **Tina**.
Is Tina **working**?	No, she **isn't working**.
What is Tina doing?	She is **camping by the lake**.
Are you **staying** by the lake?	No, I'm not.
Where are you staying?	I am staying **at the park**.

Questions in the present continuous tense are used to ask about what is happening now.

In present continuous questions the subject comes after the verb *to be*.

to be + subject + **-*ing* form**

Add question words like *who*, *what*, *where*, and *when* before the verb *to be* to ask for specific information.

Do not use the present participle (*-ing* form) in short answers.

Workbook 1 • Lesson 14: Traveling

Exercises

A: Write the **negative statement** in the **present continuous** tense. Use the **same subject**.

1. Tim and I do not plan the trips.   *Tim and I are not planning the trips.*
2. We do not pack a tent.   _____
3. Mary does not drive to school.   _____
4. I do not start at the park.   _____
5. You do not finish at the beach.   _____
6. Robert does not stay at the lake.   _____
7. Sheila does not leave today.   _____
8. You do not help.   _____
9. The computer does not work.   _____
10. I do not keep old gloves.   _____

B: Change the present continuous statement to a **present continuous question**. Use <u>subject pronouns.</u>

1. Ashley is traveling north along the river.   *Is <u>she</u> traveling north along the river?*
2. Tim is driving backward.   _____
3. The boys are meeting at the river.   _____
4. My sisters and I are packing for a trip.   _____
5. A train is coming through the tunnel.   _____
6. Our family is going to the mall.   _____
7. The bus is leaving the station.   _____
8. The taxis are going below the building.   _____
9. Walter is moving south.   _____
10. You are changing the route.   _____

basicesl.com/workbook-1/lesson-14

Exercises

C: Write yes and no answers in the **present continuous** tense. Use <u>subject pronouns</u>. Follow the example.

1. Are you and Al leaving now? *Yes, <u>we</u> **are leaving** now.*

   *No, <u>we</u> **are not leaving** now.*

2. Is Jane visiting grandmother today? _____

   _____

3. Are the girls moving forward? _____

   _____

4. Are you planning for tomorrow? _____

   _____

5. Is Steven playing at the park? _____

   _____

D: Ask the question for the given answer.

1. *What Is Tom getting?* _____ Tom is getting **a tent**.
2. _____ Ann is going **to the park**.
3. _____ I prefer **the small park**.
4. _____ I am leaving **in one hour**.
5. _____ Pete likes **the red jacket**.
6. _____ **Jane** is traveling.
7. _____ **No, they aren't** driving north.
8. _____ Jen is going **to the beach**.
9. _____ I am starting **today**.
10. _____ Jane is meeting **her sister**.

Exercises

E: Complete the sentences with the **present** or **present continuous** tense. Use the *clues* in the sentences.

I __*am visiting*__ Yellowstone Park *this week*. The park is in northwest Wyoming. My
    to visit

Uncle George _____ and _____ here at the park. *Right now*, I
            to live   *to work*

_____ at the park map. My uncle and I _____ *tonight* near a big lake.
  to look   *to camp*

My uncle _____ the route.
          to know

My sister Ellen and her friend _____ in Yosemite Park *this week*. Yosemite is near
                                      to stay

the middle of California. Ellen _____ the mountains. Right now, Ellen and her
                                  to love

friend _____ to the park. They _____ close to the mountains.
        to drive   *to get*

My brother Dan _____ *this week*. He _____ a trip to the Grand
                 to travel (not)   *to plan*

Canyon. Dan _____ a new backpack for the trip.
           to need

F: Write a negative and affirmative statement. Use the given clues. Follow the example.

1. Ashley travels on the train.   *Ashley **isn't talking** on the train.*

   (to talk, to sleep)   ***She's sleeping** on the train.*

2. The students sit in the classroom.   _____

   (to work, to learn)   _____

3. My friends and I camp in the mountains.   _____

   (to live, to travel)   _____

4. I shop for clothes at the mall.   _____

   (to sell, to buy)   _____

5. You don't like the beach.   _____

   (to stay, to leave)   _____

basicesl.com/workbook-1/lesson-14

Exercises

G: Follow the example.

1. Jane / to travel / lake

Is Jane traveling to the beach?

No, she isn't traveling to the beach.

***Where** is she traveling?*

*She's traveling to the **lake**.*

2. Albert / to talk / woman

3. taxi / to go / south

4. boys / to visit / lake

5. Tim and I / to take / train

Workbook 1 • Lesson 14: Traveling

Exercises

H: Listen to the story and choose the correct answer.
Visit **basicesl.com/workbook-1/lesson-14** to listen to the story.

1. Mary is in the __school library__ right now.

        a. city library   (**b.**) school library   **c.** church

2. Mary _____ right now.

        a. is studying   **b.** isn't studying   **c.** isn't finishing

3. Mary is looking for a book at the _____ of the library.

        a. front   **b.** middle   **c.** back

4. Mary wants a book about _____.

        a. mountains   **b.** lakes   **c.** rivers

5. Mary is _____ a trip with her family.

        a. planning   **b.** finishing   **c.** staying

6. Dave is at the _____ right now.

        a. post office   **b.** church   **c.** mall

7. Dave is shopping for a _____ .

        a. new scarf   **b.** new gloves   **c.** new jacket

8. Dave needs help from the _____ .

        a. customer   **b.** salesperson   **c.** children

basicesl.com/workbook-1/lesson-14

Lesson 15

Directions

Imperative statements

Asking for direction

 basicesl.com/workbook-1/lesson-15

- ☐ Watch vocabulary video. Listen and repeat.
- ☐ Complete vocabulary exercises. (**Download**)
- ☐ Watch grammar video. Listen and repeat.
- ☐ Complete grammar exercises. (**Workbook**)
- ☐ Complete extra grammar exercises. (**Download**)
- ☐ Take a quiz. (**Download**)

Vocabulary

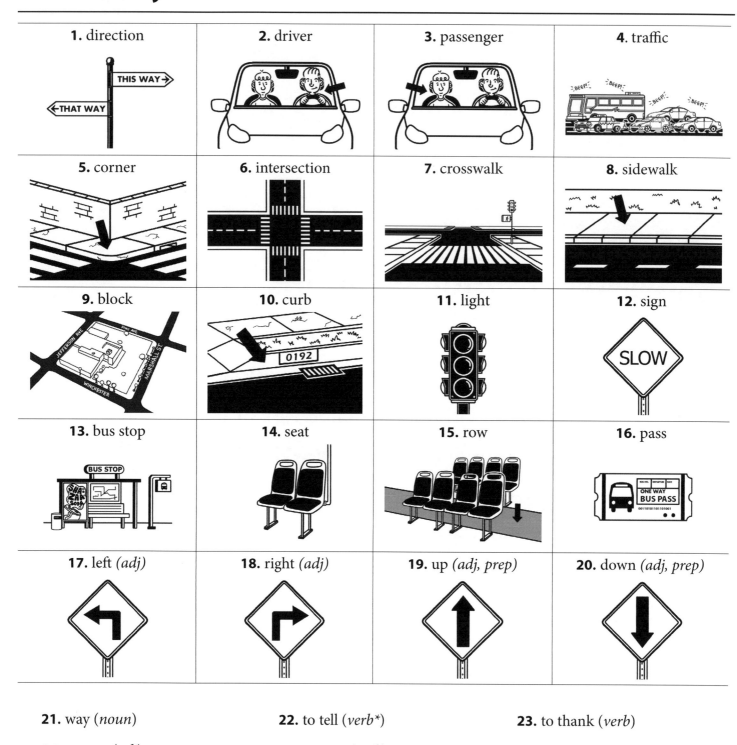

21. way (*noun*)
22. to tell (*verb**)
23. to thank (*verb*)
24. to stop (*adj*)
25. to turn (*verb*)
26. to cross (*verb*)
27. to wait (*verb*)
28. to pass (*verb*)
29. to let (*verb**)

* *Irregular verb list page 6*

Grammar

Imperative statements

Command
Get in the taxi.
Stop at the traffic light.
Pass through the intersection.
Ask for directions.
Walk that way.

Negative command
Don't **get** in the taxi.
Don't **stop** at the traffic light.
Don't **pass** through the intersection.
Don't **ask** for directions.
Don't **walk** that way.

Polite command
Please **turn** at the corner.
Please **pass** the next bus stop.
Please **stand** by the sign.
Please **wait** at the crosswalk.
Please **use** my bus pass.

Polite negative command
Please don't **turn** at the corner.
Please don't **pass** the next bus stop.
Please don't **stand** by the sign.
Please don't **wait** at the crosswalk.
Please don't **use** my bus pass.

Suggestion
Let's go home after school.
Let's walk around.
Let's cross the street now.
Let's sit in the third row.

Negative suggestion
Let's not **go** home after school.
Let's not **walk** around.
Let's not **cross** the street now.
Let's not **sit** in the third row.

Imperative sentences are used to make statements like commands, suggestions or directions.

The subject of an imperative sentence is always *you*. The subject *you* is **not** in the sentence.

Imperative sentences like commands begin with the **base form** of the **main verb**.

Negative commands use the words *do not* or *don't* before the main verb.

Polite commands use the word *please* before or after the command.

Suggestions use the words *let's* or *let's not* before the main verb. *Let's* is the contraction of the words *let* and *us*.

Asking for directions

Question
Which way is the bus going?
Which way is the train going?
Which way is your house?
Which way is the bank?

Answer
The bus is going **north**.
The train is going **south**.
My house is **straight up the hill**.
The bank is **that way**.

Question
Which way *is* the hospital?

Answer
Go down M Street.
Turn left at the light.
Walk three blocks to 3rd Street.
Cross along the crosswalk.
The hospital is **on the corner**.

To ask for directions use the question words *which way* followed by the verb *to be*.

It is common to use imperatives to give directions.

Workbook 1 • Lesson 15: Directions

Exercises

A: Write a positive **command**, **polite command** or **suggestion**. Use contractions. Follow the example.

1. **command** to turn-left-M Street   *Turn* left on M Street.

2. **suggestion** to turn-right-light   *Let's turn* right at the light.

3. **polite command** to stop-light   _____

4. **command** to cross-next-street   _____

5. **command** to get on-second-bus   _____

6. **polite command** to wait-next-bus   _____

7. **command** to drive-north-post office   _____

8. **suggestion** to go-backward   _____

9. **polite command** to thank-passenger   _____

10. **suggestion** to plan-trip   _____

B: Write a **negative command**, **polite command** or **suggestion**. Use contractions. Follow the example.

1. **command** to get off-first-bus stop   *Don't get off* at the first bus stop.

2. **suggestion** to visit-castle-today   *Let's not visit* the castle today.

3. **polite command** to pass-next-car   _____

4. **command** to go-forward.   _____

5. **suggestion** to put-car-garage   _____

6. **polite command** to go-down-G Street   _____

7. **command** to use-my-car   _____

8. **suggestion** to ask-driver-directions   _____

9. **polite command** to stop - corner   _____

10. **suggestion** to drive-sidewalk   _____

basicesl.com/workbook-1/lesson-15

Exercises

C: Write positive and negative statements. Use contractions. Follow the example.

1. **command** **to wait** / bus / train

   Wait for the bus. ***Don't wait*** *for the train.*

2. **suggestion** **to walk** / one block / two blocks

   Let's walk one block. ***Let's not walk*** *two blocks.*

3. **polite command** **to cross** / M Street / G Avenue

   _____

4. **command** **to share** / jackets / underwear

   _____

5. **suggestion** **to turn** / left / right

   _____

6. **polite command** **to go** / bridge / railroad

   _____

7. **command** **to write** / pencil / pen

   _____

8. **suggestion** **to get on** / bus 42 / bus 57

   _____

9. **polite command** **to buy** / these hats / those socks

   _____

10. **command** **to take** / jacket / sweater

    _____

Workbook 1 • Lesson 15: Directions

Exercises

D: Read the dialogue and answer the questions. Use complete sentences. Follow the example.

Jim: Which way is Jefferson Park from here?

Jessica: Jefferson Park is on Washington Avenue. We are at the corner of Main Street and Broadway Avenue. You need to cross the river. Don't use the bridge on Main Street. It is closed. Walk three blocks south on Broadway Avenue. Turn right at the computer store on Third Street. Walk five blocks and cross the bridge. After the bridge turn left at Washington Avenue and walk three blocks. The park is on the right side of the street.

1. What does Jim ask Jessica for?

He asks Jessica for directions to Jefferson Park.

2. Where is the park?

3. Where are Jim and Jessica?

4. What is closed?

5. Where does Jim turn right?

6. Where does Jim turn left?

7. Which side of the street is the park on?

basicesl.com/workbook-1/lesson-15

Exercises

E: Complete the directions with the lesson vocabulary and the map below.

church → post office / walk + red bus

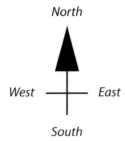

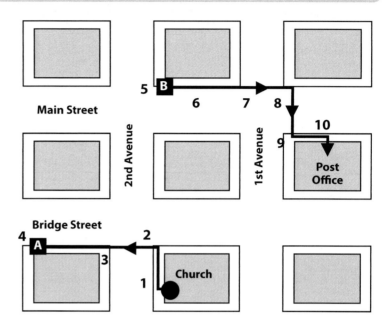

1. Walk to the ___corner___ of Bridge Street and ___2nd___ Avenue.

2. Turn _____ and _____ 2nd Avenue.

3. Walk _____ one _____.

4. _____ on the red bus at bus stop _____.

5. Get _____ the red bus at bus stop _____.

6. Go _____ one block on _____ Street.

7. _____ 1st Avenue.

8. Turn _____ and cross _____ Street.

9. Turn _____ and walk _____ on Main Street.

10. The _____ is on your _____.

Workbook 1 • Lesson 15: Directions

Exercises

F: Listen to the story and choose the correct answer.
Visit **basicesl.com/workbook-1/lesson-15** to listen to the story.

1. The man wants directions to the ___courthouse___ .

    a. bank   **b.** post office   **c.** courthouse

2. Is the courthouse far?

    a. Yes   **b.** No

3. Is the courthouse near the post office?

    a. Yes   **b.** No

4. First, the man needs to drive _____ three blocks.

    a. east   **b.** west   **c.** south

5. The man needs to turn _____ at Washington St.

    a. left   **b.** right

4. First, the man needs cross the _____ .

    a. street   **b.** freeway   **c.** bridge

7. The man needs to turn _____ at Court St.

    a. left   **b.** right

8. The _____ of the courthouse is on Court St.

    a. front   **b.** back   **c.** side

Workbook 1 • Lessons 1-15
basicesl.com/workbook-1

Answer Key

SESMA
BilingualDictionaries.com

Lesson 1

Lesson 1

Exercise A

1. sisters
2. aunts
3. husbands
4. nephews
5. friends
6. nieces
7. brothers
8. names
9. mothers
10. cousins
11. fathers
12. daughters

Exercise B

1. a
2. an
3. a
4. a
5. a
6. a
7. a
8. a
9. a
10. a
11. an
12. a

Exercise C

1. she
2. they
3. they
4. he
5. she
6. you
7. it
8. we

Exercise D

1. is
2. are
3. is
4. are
5. are
6. am
7. is
8. are

Exercise E

1. The **wife** of **Henry** is Sarah.
2. The **sister** of **Anthony** is Amy.
3. The **children** of Henry and **Sarah** are Ray and Lily.
4. The **parents** of Sarah and **Betty** are **Gary** and Carmen.
5. The **brother** of Lily is Ray.
6. The **cousins** of Lily are **Amy** and Anthony.
7. The **grandparents** of Amy are **Gary** and **Carmen**.
8. The **uncle** of Lily and **Ray** is Jose.

Exercise F

1. My name is Katie.
   I am a sister.
   I am the sister of Betty.
2. My name is Diana.
   I am an aunt.
   I am the aunt of Eric.
3. My name is Walter.
   I am a son.
   I am the son of William.
4. My name is Paula.
   I am a wife.
   I am the wife of Bob.
5. I am Julian.
   I am an uncle.
   I am the uncle of Taylor.

Lesson 2

Exercise G

1. is	12. is
2. are	13. am
3. is	14. are
4. am	15. are
5. is	16. are
6. are	17. are
7. is	18. are
8. am	19. are
9. is	20. is
10. is	21. are
11. am	22. are

Exercise H

1. The sisters **are** from Mexico. Jane is **a** friend of my brother. Jenny is **an** aunt. She is the aunt of my cousin.

2. My name **is** Ben. I **am** a grandson. My father is **the** son of my grandfather. My sister is the **daughter** of my father. My mother is **the** wife of my father. I am the son of my mother.

3. **We** are cousins. The name of our grandmother **is** Cecilia Gomez. We **are** from the United States. My last name **is** Jennings. **The** last name of my cousins **is** Campos.

Exercise I

My name is Tim. My family is from Mexico. Tony is my brother. Mary is my aunt. Steve is my uncle. Aunt Mary and Uncle Steve are also from Mexico. My cousins are Jane and Julia. They are sisters.

1. a. Mexico	4. a. aunt
2. b. brother	5. b. sisters
3. b. uncle	6. c. cousins

Lesson 2

Exercise A

1. mean	10. fat
2. short	11. serious
3. ugly	12. young
4. confident	13. nice
5. single	14. sad
6. ugly	15. bad
7. ugly	16. beautiful
8. tall	17. skinny
9. polite	18. good

Exercise B

1. husband	6. grandfather
2. uncle	7. son
3. nephew	8. brother-in-law
4. father	9. grandson
5. brother	

Exercise C

1. the	7. a
2. a	8. an
3. the	9. a
4. the	10. the
5. the	11. an
6. a	12. a

Lesson 2

Exercise D

1. They are short.
2. She is not ugly.
3. It is beautiful.
4. He is confident.
5. He is single.
6. They are handsome.
7. She is shy.
8. He is old.
9. She is skinny.
10. They are polite.
11. We are smart.
12. We are not happy.
13. You are sad.
14. He is honest.
15. They are sad.
16. He/She is not married.
17. He is married
18. She is funny.
19. He is short.
20. They are from China.
21. We are brothers.
22. You are married.

Exercise E

1. She is not mean.
2. You are not short.
3. She is not ugly.
4. I am not married.
5. He is not sad.
6. They are not fat.
7. We are not ugly.

Exercise F

1. Pat and Steven are tall.
2. The nephew is shy.
3. You are not rude.
4. What is Mary like?
5. I am tall and handsome.
6. The brother is not happy.
7. He is not my brother.

Exercise G

1. is
2. is not
3. is
4. is not
5. are
6. are not
7. are
8. are not
9. is
10. is not
11. are
12. are not

Exercise H

1. What is Tom like?
   He is skinny.
   He is not fat.
2. What is Aunt Mary like?
   She is old.
   She is not young.
3. What are Jim and Carol like?
   They are married.
   They are not single.
4. What are you like?
   I am tall.
   I am not short.
5. What are the sisters like?
   They are beautiful.
   They are not ugly.
6. What am I like?
   You are funny.
   You are not serious.

Lesson 3

Exercise I

I am Paul. Mary is my niece. She is young and beautiful. Mary is married to Peter. Peter is tall and handsome. They are happy.

John is my nephew. John is also tall and handsome. He is single.

Sara and Ann are my sisters. Sara is the mother of Mary. Ann is the mother of John. Sara is polite. Ann is shy.

1. a. niece
2. b. young
3. b. married
4. c. nephew
5. b. single
6. a. sisters
7. a. polite
8. c. shy

Lesson 3

Exercise A

1. My
2. Your
3. Our
4. His
5. Her
6. Its
7. Their
8. Your
9. Our
10. Their
11. His
12. My
13. Your
14. Her

Exercise B

1. is
2. am
3. are
4. are
5. is
6. is
7. am
8. are
9. is
10. is
11. is
12. is
13. are
14. are

Exercise C

1. nice
2. ugly
3. old
4. skinny / thin
5. rude
6. beautiful / handsome
7. happy
8. good
9. tall
10. shy

Exercise D

1. She's twelve years old.
2. I'm with the guests.
3. They're excited.
4. We're brothers.
5. You're an aunt.
6. He's with my uncle.
7. It's my birthday.
8. She's my mother.
9. He's confident and handsome.
10. I'm sorry.

Exercise E

1. We're not young.
2. He isn't old.
3. It's not fun.
4. They aren't with her family.
5. You're not my brother.
6. Tim and I aren't shy.
7. It isn't her birthday.
8. Jane and Mary aren't happy.
9. We aren't angry.
10. I'm not with Jerry.

Lesson 3

Exercise F

1. She is not five years old
   She's not five years old
   She isn't five years old
2. You are not eleven years old.
   You're not eleven years old.
   You aren't eleven years old.
3. They are not big gifts.
   They're not big gifts.
   They aren't big gifts.
4. It is not with my family.
   It's not with my family.
   It isn't with my family.
5. We are not twelve years old.
   We're not twelve years old.
   We aren't twelve years old.
6. I am not fifty years old.
   I'm not fifty years old.

Exercise G

1. What is Mary like?
   She isn't old.
   She's young.
2. What are John and Jose like?
   They aren't ugly.
   They're handsome.
3. What is the cake like?
   It isn't small.
   It's big.
4. What are Gina and I like?
   You aren't boring.
   You're fun.
5. What are you and Sara like?
   We aren't shy.
   We're confident.
6. What are you like?
   I am not mean.
   I'm nice.

Exercise H

   Tom is my friend. **He's** thirteen years old. **He** is a teenager. **He isn't** an adult.
   His birthday party is fun. It **isn't** boring. **His** cake is big. **It's** not small.
   I'm with **Tom** and **his** cousins. **His** cousins are Jane and Lee. **They're** nice. They **aren't** mean.
   The guests of **Tom** are happy and excited. **His** guests **aren't** mean and rude.

Exercise I

   Tom is my friend. He is fifteen years old. It's his birthday. His family is from Mexico. He's here with with his mother, father and brothers. His brother Tony is twelve years old. His brother John is eight years old. Their parents are old and happy.
   Tom and his family are fun. His grandfather and grandmother are from Spain. They are nice. They aren't mean. The grandmother isn't shy. The grandfather is funny.

1. c. fifteen
2. b. Mexico
3. a. brothers
4. b. twelve
5. a. eight
6. b. boring
7. a. shy
8. c. funny

Lesson 4

Exercise A

1. love	7. loves
2. love	8. love
3. loves	9. loves
4. loves	10. loves
5. love	11. loves
6. love	12. love

Exercise B

1. his	7. our
2. his	8. their
3. his/her	9. our
4. your	10. your
5. my	11. our
6. their	12. her

Exercise C

1. He's in the classroom.
2. They're in the restroom.
3. I'm in the library.
4. She's in the office.
5. You're in the cafeteria.
6. It's in the school.

Exercise D

1. sits	11. play
2. stand	12. plays
3. talks	13. sit
4. loves	14. like
5. learn	15. hugs
6. laughs	16. likes
7. stands	17. runs
8. love	18. run
9. learn	19. talk
10. laugh	20. talk

Exercise E

Kathryn and Holly are students. **They're** smart and polite. **They're** sixteen years old. **They're not (They aren't)** from the United States. **They're** from France.

Kathryn and Holly learn English at their school. **Their** teacher is Mrs. Gonzalez. **Kathryn and Holly sit** with **their** friends in the classroom. **They listen** to **their** teacher.

Exercise F

1. Where is the coach?
   He's (She's) in the gym.
   The coach runs in the gym.
2. Where are the boys?
   They're in the classroom.
   The boys learn in the classroom.
3. Where are we?
   We're in the library.
   We laugh in the library.
4. Where are the students?
   They're in the cafeteria.
   The students sit in the cafeteria.
5. Where is Mark?
   He's in the office.
   Mark talks in the office.
6. Where are you?
   I'm at the school.
   I teach at the school.

Lesson 4

Exercise G

1. Mary is in the classroom.
   She learns with her classmates.
2. We are in (at) the library.
   We sit with our teachers.
3. The coach is in the gym.
   He (She) runs with his (her) students.
4. The girls are on the playground.
   They play with their friends.
5. The students are in the office.
   They talk with their principal.

Exercise H

My name is Dan. I love my school. My school isn't old. It's new. My teacher is nice. She teaches in my classroom. My friend Amy isn't in my class. She learns in the library.

   Amy and I sit and talk in the cafeteria. The playground is fun. Our classmates run and laugh on the playground. The teachers sit in the office.

1. c. loves
2. b. new
3. c. nice
4. a. library
5. b. cafeteria
6. a. fun
7. a. classmates
8. c. sit

Lesson 5

Exercise A

1. do
2. does
3. does
4. do
5. does
6. do
7. does
8. do
9. do
10. do
11. does
12. do

Exercise B

1. I do not love math.
2. You do not read French.
3. He does not understand science.
4. She does not know the answer.
5. Jim does not ask questions.
6. It does not play music.
7. We do not like art.
8. They do not study history.

Exercise C

1. don't
2. don't
3. doesn't
4. doesn't
5. doesn't
6. don't
7. doesn't
8. don't
9. doesn't
10. doesn't
11. don't
12. don't

Exercise D

1. Lucy does not write in English. Her English teacher is not good.
2. Tim does not like math and science. Math is not easy.
3. Ray does not read in the classroom. The teacher is not serious.
4. She does not love music. Music is not fun.
5. We do not study in the library. The librarian is not nice.
6. The girls do not love art. It is not easy.

Lesson 5

Exercise E

1. Three plus three equals six.
2. Four times (multiplied by) two equals six.
3. Five minus zero equals five.
4. Six divided by two equals three.
5. Twelve minus one equals eleven.
6. Two times (multiplied by) ten equals twenty.
7. Thirteen minus four equals nine.
8. Fifteen divided by three equals five.

Exercise F

1. How old is Kathy?
   She's twelve years old.
   Kathy likes history.
   She doesn't like art.
2. How old are the girls?
   They're nine years old.
   The girls study math.
   They don't study health.
3. How old is the boy?
   He's eleven years old.
   The boy loves science.
   He doesn't love tests.
4. How old is Pam?
   She's seven years old.
   Pam writes the answer.
   She doesn't write the question.
5. How old is Tom?
   He's eight years old.
   Tom knows geography.
   He doesn't know music.

Exercise G

Pam **is not** my friend. She **is not** twelve years old. She **does not like** art and history. She **does not read** history with her teacher.

Pam **does not love** her teacher. Mrs. Brown **is not** from England. She **is not** twenty-five years old.

Pam **is not** smart. She **does not write** in her English class. She **does not ask** questions in her classroom. She **does not learn** Spanish at school.

Lucy **is not** a friend of Pam. She **does not like** math and science. Pam and Lucy **do not sit** together on the playground.

Exercise H

My name is Ray. I am fifteen years old. I like art and music. Art is beautiful. Music is fun. I don't like math. Math is difficult to understand.

My friend Pam loves math and science. She doesn't understand art. Pam comes from a big family. They are from China. They speak Chinese. Pam is sixteen years old.

Her friend Lucy isn't very confident. She is not good at tests. Lucy doesn't like history class. Lucy speaks Spanish. She learns English with her friends and teacher.

1. a. fifteen
2. b. art
3. a. math
4. b. difficult
5. c. science
6. b. understand
7. b. China
8. b. Chinese
9. b. sixteen
10. c. confident
11. a. history
12. c. English

Lesson 6

Lesson 6

Exercise A

1. have
2. has
3. have
4. has
5. has
6. have
7. has
8. have
9. has
10. has
11. have
12. have

Exercise B

1. go
2. goes
3. go
4. goes
5. go
6. go
7. go
8. goes
9. go
10. goes
11. go
12. go

Exercise C

1. The question does show an answer.
   The question doesn't show an answer.
2. I do want my ruler.
   I don't want my ruler.
3. She does have two notebooks.
   She doesn't have two notebooks.
4. It does correct the tests.
   It doesn't correct the tests.

Exercise D

1. She goes to the classroom.
2. He learns in the classroom.
3. John has three pens.
4. I have a ruler.
5. We are in the cafeteria.
6. I am not at your desk.
7. They aren't difficult.
8. You and Mary are not happy.
9. We aren't in the cafeteria.
10. I want a chair.
11. It doesn't have mistakes.
12. Tom doesn't use glue.
13. I don't correct the papers.
14. He doesn't like history class.
15. She doesn't remember our grades.
16. Jimmy does speak Chinese.
17. I do know French.
18. Sarah does have five books.
19. You do have a marker.
20. You do have paper.

Exercise E

1. Mike doesn't have a pen.
   He does have pencils.
   He has three pencils.
2. The girls don't have glue.
   They do have rulers.
   They have four rulers.
3. The student doesn't go to the library.
   He does go to class.
   He goes to one class.
4. The boys don't play in the gymnasium.
   They do play on the playgrounds.
   They play on the two playgrounds.
5. I don't understand the exercise.
   I do understand the lessons.
   I understand the five lessons.

Lesson 7

Exercise F
She likes her school. **She goes** to school with her friends. **She has** two good friends. **Her friends** are Josh and Ashley. **She has** one class with Josh. **She doesn't have** a class with Ashley.

She doesn't go to the playground with Ashley. **She does** go to the playground with Josh.

She understands her history lesson. **She doesn't** understand **her** math lesson. **She doesn't** use **her** geography book. **She does** use **her** science book.

Exercise G
1. Eight plus thirteen equals twenty-one.
2. Three times (multiplied by) zero equals zero.
3. Fourteen times (multiplied by) one equals fourteen.
4. Eighteen divided by two equals nine.
5. Fifteen minus seven equals eight.
6. Twelve divided by one equals twelve.
7. Twenty-nine minus twenty-eight equals one.
8. Fifteen plus twelve equals twenty-seven.

Exercise H
My name is Alan. Greg is my cousin. Greg goes to my school. Greg likes art. He doesn't like math. Math is difficult for him. Greg forgets his math lessons.

Greg has a desk and a chair in his classroom. He has two pencils and a notebook on his desk. The teacher has a computer on her desk. Greg doesn't have a computer on his desk. He does have scissors and glue in his desk.

Our school is big. It has a library, a gym and an auditorium. Greg goes to the library in the morning. Greg doesn't study in the library. He talks to his friends. Greg remembers the map in the library from his geography class. The map is beautiful.

1. a. cousin
2. b. art
3. a. math
4. c. pencils
5. a. computer
6. a. does have
7. b. library
8. b. doesn't study
9. a. talks
10. a. geography

Lesson 7

Exercise A
1. Is Mary in the kitchen?
2. Are the windows open?
3. Is the balcony big?
4. Are you on the balcony?
5. Are the desks in the classrooms?
6. Is Henry in the garage?
7. Are the girls in the restroom?
8. Is the fence nice?
9. Are the doors old?
10. Is the carpet dirty?
11. Are the parents angry?
12. Is the coach serious?

Exercise B
1. Where
2. Who
3. How
4. What
5. What
6. When
7. Who
8. Where

Lesson 7

Exercise C

1. Yes, the window is small.
   Yes, it is.
2. No, the blinds aren't open.
   No, they aren't.
3. No, the fence isn't closed.
   No, it isn't.
4. Yes, the boys are in the garage.
   Yes, they are.
5. No, you aren't at my apartment.
   No, you aren't.
6. Yes, the couch is in the living room.
   Yes, it is.
7. Yes, I am downstairs.
   Yes, I am.
8. No, the chair isn't on the patio.
   No, it isn't.
9. No, the scissors aren't in the kitchen.
   No, they aren't.
10. Yes, the bathroom is dirty.
    Yes, it is.

Exercise D

1. She's at her house in the kitchen.
2. He's at his apartment on the balcony.
3. He's with his brother and sister.
4. It's nice and clean.
5. It's on the wall in the dining room.
6. She reads books about art in her history class.

Exercise E

1. Are Tom and Alex in the dining room?
   No, they're not in the dining room.
   Where are they?
   They're in the living room.
2. Is Cynthia in the apartment?
   No, she's not in the apartment.
   Where is she?
   She's in the house.
3. Are you in the bedroom?
   No, I'm not in the bedroom.
   Where are you?
   I'm in the office.
4. Is Fred in the yard?
   No, he's not in the yard.
   Where is he?
   He's in the bathroom.
5. Is the television in the garage?
   No, it's not in the garage.
   Where is it?
   It's in the living room.

Exercise F

1. What is her name?
2. How old is Betty?
3. Who is fifty-two years old?
4. What is he like?
5. Where is she?
6. When is Raymond at his apartment?
7. Where is the couch?
8. Who is the brother of Betty?

Lesson 8

Exercise G

My name is Karen. I live in a big house with my family. Our house is old. The stairs are ugly. The windows are clean. The house has one bedroom and one bathroom downstairs. It has three bedrooms and two bathrooms upstairs. We use one bedroom as an office.

Our house has a beautiful yard. My father walks in the yard at night. My mother reads on the patio. She wants a television for the patio. My brothers play on the fence. I sit and study my lessons. We are happy here.

1. c. big
2. a. old
3. a. stairs
4. a. bedrooms
5. b. walks
6. b. patio
7. a. mother
8. c. fence

Lesson 8

Exercise A
1. Does, want
2. Does, has
3. Do, get
4. Does, goes
5. Do, put
6. Does, needs

Exercise B
1. Does John put the cup on the shelf?
2. Does Mary take the bowls to the counter?
3. Do the girls need forks?
4. Do the boys want spoons?
5. Do we wash the pots and pans?
6. Does Gina remember the old stove?
7. Does Greg get the refrigerator?
8. Do I get a knife?
9. Do you need a glass?
10. Does the cup go in the cupboard?
11. Do the napkins go in the wastebasket?
12. Does the sink have dirty plates?
13. Do you need a new oven?
14. Does Tina want your microwave?
15. Does Anne like our kitchen?

Exercise C
1. Yes, I have napkins.
   No, I don't.
2. Yes, the table needs a tablecloth.
   No, it doesn't.
3. Yes, Fred likes the plates.
   No, he doesn't.
4. Yes, the students use the oven.
   No, they don't.
5. Yes, you get a pencil.
   No, you don't.
6. Yes, Katy goes to school.
   No, she doesn't.
7. Yes, the cupboard has a shelf.
   No, it doesn't.
8. Yes, the windows have blinds.
   No, they don't.
9. Yes, the stove gets dirty.
   No, it doesn't.
10. Yes, I want another knife.
    No, I don't.
11. Yes, he goes to school.
    No, he doesn't.

Exercise D
1. Yes, the kitchen has an oven.
2. The clean cups go on the shelf.
3. The dirty plates are in the sink.
4. Yes, her sons do wash the plates.
5. The table needs a tablecloth.
6. Paula puts a fork, knife and spoon on the napkins.

Lesson 8

Exercise E

1. Does father need a cup?
   No, he doesn't need a cup.
   What does he need?
   He needs a glass.
2. Does Jan get a knife?
   No, she doesn't get a knife.
   What does she get?
   She gets a fork.
3. Do Al and Pam want a refrigerator?
   No, they don't want a refrigerator.
   What do they want?
   They want an oven.
4. Does the kitchen have a microwave?
   No, it doesn't have a microwave.
   What does it have?
   It has a stove.
5. Do I take a bowl?
   No, you don't take a bowl.
   What do I take?
   You take a plate.

Exercise F

1. Who do you get a clean plate from?
   Who gets a clean plate?
2. Who goes to the library?
   Who does Kevin go to the library with?
3. What has an eraser?
   What do the students have?
4. What do you learn in class?
   Who learns math and English?
5. Who sits at the table?
   Who do they sit at the table with?

Exercise G

Jane and her mother have a new apartment. Their kitchen is beautiful and clean. It has a refrigerator and an oven. It doesn't have a microwave.

Jane's mother uses the oven every day. Jane moves the plates from the sink to the cupboard at night. Jane's mother wants a new tablecloth for the table.

The door to the patio does not open. Jane and her mother sit at the kitchen table. Jane loves their new apartment.

1. c. sister
2. a. dressers
3. b. shelves
4. b. dirty
5. a. toothbrushes
6. b. cupboard
7. c. closet
8. b. wastebasket

Lesson 9

Exercise A

1. glasses
2. plates
3. knives
4. balconies
5. toothbrushes
6. stoves
7. coaches
8. microwaves
9. libraries
10. boys
11. wives
12. parties
13. birthdays
14. shelves
15. histories
16. glasses
17. forks
18. families
19. tables
20. couches

Lesson 9

Exercise B

1. The towel of Dave is dirty.
   Dave's towel is dirty.
2. The pillow of Donna is soft.
   Donna's pillow is soft.
3. The closets of your sister are big.
   Your sister's closets are big.
4. The bedrooms of the boys are upstairs.
   The boys' bedrooms are upstairs.
5. The dresser of the girl is in her bedroom.
   The girl's dresser is in her bedroom.

Exercise C

1. The boys need combs.
2. The trays go on the shelves.
3. They clean their bedrooms.
4. Are the toilets dirty?
5. Do the men clean the showers?
6. Are Pam's brushes in drawers?
7. Sam's toothbrushes are on the sink.
8. We take the plates to the counter.
9. My sons are at the library.
10. The libraries have books.
11. The boys sleep with the blankets.
12. They need the glasses.
13. They look for razors.
14. Alex's houses have televisions.
15. Do the couches look soft?
16. Their offices are at Frank's school.
17. Our balcony doors are closed.
18. The coaches help the teachers.
19. The men and women are here.
20. The children's gifts are at the party.
21. Do we put the knives in the drawer?
22. My sons want new towels.

Exercise D

1. Where is Tom?
2. What does Tom learn?
3. Is Tom smart?
4. What is Tom's last name?
5. How old is Tom?
6. Does Tom like art?
7. Is Jane a child?
8. How old is Jane?
9. What is Jane like?
10. Does Jane read books?
11. Where does Jane read?
12. Is Jane's bedroom downstairs?
13. Does Jane like her bedroom?
14. Who is John?
15. How old is John?
16. Do you love your brother?
17. Is John married?
18. Is John handsome?
19. Where is John's room?

Exercise E

1. Yes, her favorite rooms are the kitchen and the bedroom.
2. Her bedroom is upstairs.
3. Her home has two bathrooms.
4. She uses the toaster on the counter.
5. She puts the dirty dishes in the sink.
6. No, her bedroom isn't messy.
7. Yes, she has three blankets in the closet.

Lesson 9

Exercise F
1. My daughter's bedroom is messy.
2. My house's bedrooms are upstairs.
3. Your schools' playgrounds are fun.
4. The library's books are boring.
5. The children's cousins are polite.
6. The girls' uncle is funny.

Exercise G

Jen is Pam's sister. They have two bedrooms and one bathroom. Jen's bedroom has two beds and two dressers. It has one closet. The closet has a mirror and shelves. Jen's blankets are on the shelves.

Their bathroom is clean. A glass for toothbrushes is on the sink. The soap is in the bathtub. Pam keeps her towels in the cupboard with the toilet paper. Jen's towels are in her closet with her blankets. They need new razors. Their old razors and brushes are in the wastebasket.

1. c. sister
2. a. dressers
3. b. shelves
4. b. dirty
5. a. toothbrushes
6. b. cupboard
7. c. closet
8. b. wastebasket

Lesson 10

Exercise A
1. these
2. those
3. these
4. Those
5. That
6. this
7. those
8. this
9. these
10. That
11. This
12. That

Exercise B
1. adjective
2. pronoun
3. adjective
4. pronoun
5. adjective
6. pronoun
7. pronoun
8. adjective
9. pronoun
10. adjective
11. pronoun
12. adjective

Exercise C
1. This is a dirty hat.
2. That is an ugly jacket.
3. These are clean jeans.
4. Those are nice shoes.
5. That is an old dress.
6. This is a soft t-shirt.

Exercise D
1. That skirt is ugly.
2. Those shoes are black.
3. These T-shirts are old/used.
4. Those pajamas are dirty.
5. This closet isn't neat.
6. This jacket is big.
7. That bed is soft.
8. Those sandals aren't bad.
9. These questions are difficult.
10. This book is funny.

Lesson 11

Exercise E
1. Do you like that jacket?
2. What color is this sweater?
3. Is that your favorite suit?
4. Do you like this hat?
5. Whose sweaters are these?
6. Do you like those shoes?
7. Whose green skirt is that?
8. Are those sandals new?
9. How old are those sandals?
10. Where do you keep this robe?

Exercise F
1. Alex and Bobby's bedroom is messy.
2. Those dirty jeans on the floor are Bobby's.
3. They are on the bed.
4. Alex's underwear are black.
5. Bobby uses green towels.
6. He takes the dirty clothes downstairs to the garage.

Exercise G
1. Do the boys wear these clothes?
   No, they don't wear these clothes.
   What clothes do the boys wear?
   They wear those clothes.
2. Does Cynthia hate these sandals?
   No, she doesn't hate these sandals.
   What sandals does Cynthia hate?
   She hates those sandals.
3. Do you prefer those shorts?
   No, I don't prefer those shorts.
   What shorts do you prefer?
   I prefer these shorts.
4. Does Robert choose this suit?
   No, he doesn't choose this suit.
   What suit does Robert choose?
   He chooses that suit.
5. Do I take that robe?
   No, you don't take that robe.
   What robe do I take?
   You take this robe.

Exercise H
Tanya loves her new clothes. She shares old jeans and sweaters with her sister Gina. She doesn't share her new clothes. Gina loses Tanya's old clothes.

Gina loves Tanya's closet. Tanya has new clothes in her closet. Tanya has a new orange skirt. It's her favorite skirt. Gina wants that orange skirt. It goes with her white sandals.

1. b. clothes
2. b. shares
3. c. new
4. a. loses
5. b. closet
6. c. skirt
7. b. orange
8. a. sandals

Lesson 11

Exercise A
1. b. ones
2. b. ones
3. a. one
4. a. one
5. b. ones
6. a. one
7. b. ones
8. a. one
9. a. one
10. b. ones

Lesson 11

Exercise B

1. first
2. second
3. third
4. fourth
5. fifth
6. sixth
7. seventh
8. eighth
9. ninth
10. tenth
11. eleventh
12. twelfth
13. thirty-third
14. forty-first
15. ninety-ninth
16. seventy-second
17. eighty-sixth
18. thirteenth
19. twenty-second
20. eighteenth

Exercise C

1. Which scarf does Ann want?
   She wants the fancy one.
2. Which suits do Jim and Mike share?
   They share the striped ones.
3. Which jacket do you like?
   I like the red one.
4. Which buttons do I get?
   You get the large ones.
5. Which earrings does Sara need?
   She needs the small ones.

Exercise D

1. She doesn't wear white ones.
2. We don't like your old one.
3. I don't use my new one.
4. They don't need difficult ones.
5. It doesn't go in the little one.
6. She doesn't keep her ugly ones.
7. He doesn't have tight ones.
8. You don't erase the correct ones.
9. You don't have the serious one.
10. I don't sleep in a big one.

Exercise E

My **sisters have** two closets. **They have** a large closet and a small **one**. **They keep their** favorite dresses in the large closet. They keep their favorite sweaters in the small **one**.

My **sisters'** favorite dresses are the solid **ones**. **They wear** the solid dresses to school. They do not wear the fancy **ones** to school.

My **sisters** also **love** sandals. **They have** brown sandals, black sandals, and white **ones**. The black and white sandals are tight. The brown **ones** are comfortable.

My **sisters have** jeans **they don't** wear. **They don't** wear the extra small jeans. **They** also **don't** wear the torn **ones**.

Exercise F

1. Which belt does Fred like?
   Fred likes the third belt.
   He doesn't like the first one.
2. Which book do I need?
   You need the sixth book.
   You don't need the second one.

Lesson 12

3. Which scarf does Lisa want?
   Lisa wants the fifth scarf.
   She doesn't want the fourth one.
4. Which watch do Jim and I take?
   You and Jim take the seventh watch.
   You don't take the eighth one.
5. Which earing does Kelly wear?
   She wears the first one.
   She doesn't wear the second one.
6. Which lesson do you love?
   I love the seventh lesson.
   I don't love the ninth one.

Exercise G

My name is Ellen. I have three new shirts. The first shirt is formal. The second one is casual. The third shirt is a new t-shirt. I keep my shirts in the dresser.

The formal shirt is a solid white one. It has a collar and six black buttons. This formal shirt isn't the correct size. It's uncomfortable.

The casual one is a striped shirt. The colors are blue and red. It's comfortable. The size of the casual shirt is medium.

My new t-shirt is my favorite one. The size of the t-shirt is small. It's solid red and tight. I look good in my new t-shirt.

1. c. three
2. a. first
3. a. solid
4. b. buttons
5. b. comfortable
6. b. medium
7. c. small
8. a. tight

Lesson 12

Exercise A

1. at
2. on
3. in
4. in
5. at
6. at
7. on
8. at
9. in
10. on
11. in
12. on

Exercise B

1. bottom
2. under
3. in front of
4. without
5. up
6. above
7. on
8. after
9. expensive
10. inside
11. same
12. in the back of

Exercise C

Tom needs new shoes **for** school. His shoes are old and dirty. Tom's shoes get dirty **at** school **on** the playground. Tom keeps his old shoes **inside** the garage. Tom puts his shoes **below** a table **by** the door.

Tom buys shoes **at** the shoe store. Tom's favorite shoe store is **near** his school. The store sells shoes **for** men and women. The men's shoes are **at the back of** the store. The store also sells socks and sandals. The socks are **on** a shelf **behind** the register. The sandals are **at the front of** the store.

Lesson 12

Exercise D
1. d. a & b
2. c. on
3. c. behind
4. b. behind
5. a. between
6. b. along
7. c. beside
8. d. under or below

Exercise E
1. The price tag is **on** the shirt.
2. The salesperson is **next to (by, at)** the register.
3. The customer is **in front of** the store.
4. The woman is **in (inside)** the fitting room.
5. The scarves are **under (below)** the purses.
6. The watches are **on the top (on the)** shelf.

Exercise F
1. The register is **on** the counter.
2. The couch is **in the middle** of the room.
3. The woman is **by (near, in front of)** the mirror.
4. The salesperson is **behind** the register.
5. The shelves are **at the back** of the store **along** the wall.
6. The wastebasket is **on** the floor **next to (beside)** the counter.

Exercise G

Ruby shops at clothing stores. She likes shoes and skirts. She also likes formal dresses. A dress store near her house is her favorite. It sells expensive dresses. Stores with cheap dresses are far from Ruby's house.

Ruby shops at her favorite dress store with her mother. They walk down the aisles. They look at pretty dresses. The formal dresses are at the back of the store.

Ruby's mother helps Ruby in the fitting room. Ruby prefers a blue dress. It is on sale. Ruby's mother pays for the dress at the register. Ruby and her mother walk home.

1. a. formal
2. c. near
3. b. expensive
4. b. far from
5. a. mother
6. b. at the back
7. a. on sale
8. c. pays

Lesson 13

Exercise A
1. walking
2. coming
3. learning
4. loving
5. reading
6. getting
7. forgetting
8. doing
9. working
10. driving
11. sitting
12. selling
13. buying
14. needing
15. playing
16. picking
17. putting
18. sharing
19. writing
20. wearing
21. preferring
22. beginning

Lesson 13

Exercise B

1. I am grabbing
2. You are studying
3. He is wearing
4. She is living
5. It is standing
6. We are adding
7. They are laughing
8. I am getting
9. You are listening
10. He is choosing
11. She is putting
12. It is helping
13. We are sleeping
14. They are answering
15. I am talking
16. You are writing
17. He is looking
18. She is shopping
19. It is cleaning
20. We are forming
21. They are closing
22. I am opening

Exercise C

1. I am walking to school now.
2. You are driving to church now.
3. He is riding a train now.
4. She is working in a hospital now.
5. We are living near the train station now.
6. They are shopping at the dress store now.
7. The taxi is going over the bridge now.
8. Ray is walking along the railroad now.

Exercise D

1. Tom works at the restaurant on weekends.
   He is working at the restaurant today.
2. Mary walks to the mall on Mondays.
   She is walking to the mall this morning.
3. I go to the station at 10:00 a.m.
   I am going to the station now.
4. Sarah and Jan help at the hospital on Fridays.
   They are helping at the hospital today.

Exercise E

I **am going** to the mall today with my mother and sister. We **are driving** to the train station. We **are taking** the train to the mall. We **are riding** the train through a tunnel and over a bridge. I **am sitting** next to the window today. My sister **is standing** by the door. My mother **is reading** her book on the train today.

My mother **is going** to church with her friend **today**. They **are helping** at the church **today**. My mother **is teaching** English to children from different countries. My mother's friend **is taking** people to the hospital from the church today. They **are riding** in a bus across the city.

Exercise F

1. Where does your aunt work?
   My aunt works at the courthouse.
   She's working at the courthouse now.
2. Where does Henry go?
   Henry goes to the church.
   He's going to the church now.
3. Where do you walk?
   I walk to the mall.
   I'm walking at to the mall now.
4. Where do Ann and Al study?
   Ann and Al study at the school.
   They're studying at the school now.
5. Where does Sylvia drive?
   Sylvia drives on the freeway.
   She's driving on the freeway now.
6. Where does the train go?
   The train goes through the tunnel.
   It's going through the tunnel now.

Lesson 13

Exercise G

Henry and his wife ride the train to the city. They work at the courthouse every day. Today, the train did not come. Henry and his wife are taking a taxi now. They are taking the freeway to the courthouse.

Henry's children, Alex and Susan, ride the bus to school. The children's school is far from their house. They are driving over the bridge today. Alex has a test in his first class. He is studying for the test on the bus.

1. c. train
2. b. courthouse
3. a. come
4. a. taxi
5. b. bus
6. a. far from
7. c. bridge
8. b. studying

Lesson 14

Exercise A

1. Tim and I are not planning the trips.
2. We are not packing now.
3. Mary is not driving to school.
4. I am not starting at the park.
5. You are not finishing at the beach.
6. Robert is not staying at the lake.
7. Sheila is not leaving today.
8. You are not helping.
9. The computer is not working.
10. I am not keeping torn gloves.

Exercise B

1. Is she traveling north?
2. Is he driving backward?
3. Are they meeting at the river?
4. Are we packing for a trip?
5. Is it coming through the tunnel?
6. Are we going to the mall?
7. Is it leaving the station?
8. Are they going below the building?
9. Is he moving south?
10. Are you changing the route?

Exercise C

1. Yes, we are leaving now.
   No, we are not leaving now.
2. Yes, she is visiting grandmother today.
   No, she is not visiting grandmother today.
3. Yes, they are moving forward.
   No, they are not moving forward.
4. Yes, I am planning for tomorrow.
   No, I am not planning for tomorrow.
5. Yes, he is playing at the park.
   No, he is not playing at the park.

Exercise D

1. What is Tom getting?
2. Where is Ann going?
3. Which park do you prefer?
4. When are you leaving?
5. Which jacket does Pete like?
6. What is Jane doing?
7. Are they driving north?
8. Where is Jen going?
9. When are you starting?
10. Who is Jane meeting?

Lesson 14

Exercise E

I **am visiting** Yellowstone Park this week. The park is in northwest Wyoming. My Uncle George **lives** and **works** here at the park. Right now, I **am looking** at the park map. My uncle and I **are camping** tonight near a big lake. My uncle **knows** the route.

My sister Ellen and her friend **are staying** in Yosemite Park this week. Yosemite is near the middle of California. Ellen **loves** the mountains. Right now, Ellen and her friend **are driving** to the park. They **are getting** close to the mountains.

My brother Dan **is not traveling** this week. He **is planning** a trip to the Grand Canyon. Dan **needs** a new backpack for the trip.

Exercise F

1. Ashley isn't talking on the train.
   She's sleeping on the train.
2. The students aren't working in the classroom.
   They're learning in the classroom.
3. My friends and I aren't living in the mountains.
   We're traveling in the mountains.
4. I'm not selling clothes at the mall.
   I'm buying clothes at the mall.
5. You're not staying at the beach.
   You're leaving the beach.

Exercise G

1. Is Jane traveling to the beach?
   No, she isn't traveling to the beach.
   Where is she traveling?
   She's traveling to the lake.
2. Is Albert talking to the man?
   No, he isn't talking to the man.
   Who is Albert talking to?
   He's talking to the woman.
3. Is the taxi going east?
   No, it isn't going east.
   Where is the taxi going?
   It's going south.
4. Are the boys visiting the park?
   No, they aren't visiting the park.
   Where are they visiting?
   They're visiting the lake.
5. Are Tim and I taking the bus?
   No, you aren't taking the bus.
   What are we taking?
   You're taking the train.

Lesson 14

Exercise H

Right now, Mary is finishing her day in the school library. She's not studying. She is looking for a book at the back of the library. The back shelves have history and geography books. Mary wants a good book about the Rocky Mountains. Mary is planning a trip to the Rocky Mountains with her family.

Mary's brother Dave is looking forward to his family's trip to the Rocky Mountains. Right now, Dave is shopping for a new jacket at a store in the mall. Dave needs help from a salesperson. The jackets on the racks do not have price tags. Dave likes blue and black jackets. The salesperson is coming over.

1. b. school library
2. b. isn't studying
3. c. back
4. a. mountains
5. a. planning
6. c. mall
7. c. new jacket
8. b. salesperson

Lesson 15

Exercise A

1. Turn left on (at) M Street.
2. Let's turn right at the light.
3. Please stop at the light.
4. Cross at the next street.
5. Get on the second bus.
6. Please wait for the next bus.
7. Drive north to the post office.
8. Let's go backward.
9. Please thank the passenger.
10. Let's plan a trip.

Exercise B

1. Don't get off at the first bus stop.
2. Let's not visit the castle today.
3. Please don't pass the next car.
4. Don't go forward.
5. Let's not put the car in the garage.
6. Please don't go down G Street.
7. Don't use my car.
8. Let's not ask the driver for directions.
9. Please don't stop at the corner.
10. Let's not drive on the sidewalk.

Exercise C

1. Wait for the bus. Don't wait for the train.
2. Let's walk one block. Let's not walk two blocks.
3. Please cross at M Street. Please don't cross at G Avenue.
4. Share the jackets. Don't share the underwear.
5. Let's turn left. Let's not turn right.
6. Please go to the bridge. Please don't go to the railroad.
7. Write with a pencil. Don't write with a pen.
8. Let's get on bus forty-two. Let's not get on bus fifty-seven.
9. Please buy these hats. Please don't buy those socks.
10. Take a jacket. Don't take a sweater.

Lesson 15

Exercise D

1. He asks Jessica for directions to Jefferson Park.
2. It is on Washington Avenue.
3. They are at the corner of Main Street and Broadway Avenue.
4. The bridge on Main Street is closed.
5. He turns right at the computer store on 3rd Street.
6. He turns left at Washington Avenue.
7. It is on the right side of the street.

Exercise E

1. Walk to the corner of Bridge Street and 2nd Avenue.
2. Turn left and cross 2nd Avenue.
3. Walk west one block.
4. Get on the red bus at bus stop A.
5. Get off the red bus at bus stop B.
6. Walk east one block on Main Street.
7. Cross 1st Avenue.
8. Turn right and cross Main Street.
9. Turn left and walk east on Main Street.
10. The post office is on your right.

Exercise F

Man: Hello.
Woman: Hi. How are you?
Man: I'm good. How are you?
Woman: Good, thank you. Where are you going?
Man: I am going to the courthouse. Is the courthouse far from here? Is it near the post office?
Woman: No, the courthouse is not far from here. It's not near the post office. Do you need directions?
Man: Yes please.
Woman: Drive south three blocks. Turn right on Washington Street. Drive east two blocks. Cross the bridge. Turn left on Court Street. Look for the front of the courthouse on your left.
Man: Thank you.
Woman: You're welcome.

1. c. courthouse
2. b. no
3. b. no
4. c. south
5. b. right
6. a. left
7. c. bridge
8. a. front